Friendly Fear Notebook
How to Make Fear Your Ally

Friendly Fear Notebook
How to Make Fear Your Ally

by
Lee Anne McClymont, MHA

Copyright © 2010 Lee Anne McClymont, MHA

ISBN 978-0-557-42572-3

Cover design: www.pollonidesign.com

Dear Bill,

You believed in me, friend. Thank you.

Love,

Lee Anne

A word about this tree...

Special acknowledgment goes to the many friends and family members who loved me enough to let me dare speak to you about fear. The tree on the facing page (drawn by my dear friend, artist Helen Crouse) rests as a testimony to these souls, some living and others passed. All these names invisibly swell through the pages of this book, passing on their light and love to you, the reader, because they passed on their light and love to me. What greater gift is there? Thank you. I honor all of you in word and deed. Peace.

—Lee Anne

Acknowledgments

Thank you to the creative team who worked with me to bring you this book:

Katy Koontz, the talented editor who immediately recognized the need for this message and believed in my voice to carry it. An extraordinary blend of wit and wisdom, her genius touched this manuscript through careful arrangement of chapters and kept the book a sensible length. How she managed to do this while honoring my language and tempo I may never be able to figure out.

Sherrie Wilkolaski, who from the start recognized the power of this approach and leveraged her know-how and the talent at Lulu.com to bring this book to life. Few souls are as brave in the publishing world. She sought the right venue for this work when she suggested I use Lulu.com and encouraged me through the book's slow but steady birth. Sherrie is a *visionary* who is able to discern the power of the message without tripping over the medium. *She* is where the publishing industry is going.

Alberto Polloni, life coach and graphic designer, who crafted a visual image for this work that summons the very essence of Friendly Fear: transformation. He has blessed our creative team with his leadership and people skills. We met about a year before this book was written, and after our conversation, I knew *Friendly Fear Notebook* would have the proper visual expression it demanded.

In addition, I am deeply grateful to three mental health professionals: John Chilman, M.D., psychiatrist and friend. It was "Doc Chilman" who placed within my reach a keen understanding of stress and how fear diffused can help people stay healthy. I remain ever grateful to Ms. Rivka From of To Life Coaching. Rivka is both a seasoned, executive life coach and a business coach based in Raleigh, NC. It was Rivka who gave me the space I needed to dare to grow into my own soul. Without her, *Friendly Fear Notebook* may as well have never been dreamt. Thanks also to Kerry Johnson, a licensed clinical psychotherapist in Durham, NC, who identified parallels within my work on Friendly Fear and the current treatment modalities for personality disorders. Our conversation one day last November gave me the understanding necessary for interpreting how the mind struggles with dissonance and how this struggle can dissolve once we shift our awareness. I credit the insight shared in the last chapter of this book to her incisive teaching.

Morton Coleman, M.D., is the remarkable oncologist who saved my life when I was first diagnosed with non-Hodgkin's lymphoma in 2003. He taught me how to blend *care* with *cure* and brought dignity into the treatment process so desperately sought out by humans passing through their cancer journey. God's divine arts live within his hands, heart, and soul. God bless Weill Cornell Medical College/New York-

Presbyterian Hospital for building one of the world's finest medical centers, The Center for Lymphoma and Myeloma.

The remarkable vocal artist, Mrs. Florence Peacock of Chapel Hill, NC, pushed me gently toward this book's conclusion. Without her encouragement, I may have overlooked the power of words to unravel hearts knotted in tight desperation. She is a fixed star in my constellation of heroes. Her work to preserve art and culture within the state of North Carolina and beyond marks a lifetime of achievement and love for the arts. She introduced me to America's Next Great Orchestra, the North Carolina Symphony. The concerts I listened to in Raleigh and Chapel Hill helped me to bridge the emotional gap between *hurt* and *healing*. Thank you Maestro Grant Llewellyn and the brilliant group of musicians who make up this orchestra. Music, like poetry, points the way to reconciling emotions that are too heavy to carry alone.

Mrs. Darliene Woolner of Cary, NC, helped me harmonize my dual roles of stay-at-home mother with emerging writer. We met one day for lunch when I was feeling off-track with the book's progress. She gave me a loaf of challah that day. After lunch, we walked back to our cars and I hugged her. It was the first time in my life in Raleigh that I felt my own mother's presence. Later that evening, I realized that what I encountered with Darliene was pure God-inspired Mothermind—that deep reverence for life and all the promise that it holds. I summon that spirit now with my own daughter, Emma, when she needs help. Darliene, your gifts extend beyond your remarkable grace. Thank you.

As you enter this book it may be easy to overlook the fingerprints of the brave men and women who came to one of my early workshops in Hamlet, NC. Each participant in that program helped me see the value of fear-navigation skills as they related to hope. They spoke gently, yet firmly, as they made their way through the program, "Harness Fear, Harvest Hope." Men and women arrived quietly into the conference room, each silently preparing to welcome a new truth about fear. Special thanks also to Ms. Ginger Haigler, the librarian who helped organize the program. I knew from the start that Ms. Haigler cared deeply about her patrons when, after we established the dates, she began to ask emotionally sensitive questions about the attendees' needs. Hamlet has an outstanding library in the center of town run by exceptional people.

Mrs. Gina Riggins, business coach, supported this work and understood the inherent value to people entering life transitions. Gina volunteered to accompany me on my trip to Hamlet, a six-hour drive round-trip from Raleigh. She came with me to bring the professional insight and emotional sensitivity that life and business coaches are highly sought out for. She came because, like me, she recognized that the community was in transition and knew that my workshops could be a starting point for many of the attendees. We were *all* blessed that day to have Gina help facilitate the discussions. Her feedback helped me consolidate the methods I outlined for the workshops, many of which are presented here in this book.

Mrs. Gerry Janke is my next-door neighbor. We live in a rural part of town where neighbors are spread out—sometimes acres apart. Gerry saw me struggling with the decision to move forward on this project. One day, she sat me down in her kitchen and taught me how to make a pie. I listened. I played with the piecrust dough. While the pies were baking, she passed me a cup of tea and turned to me and said in her delightful Canadian clipped speech, "Now it's your turn." I knew what she meant and nodded "yes."

My family supported me while I was writing this book. They showed me patience, love, and faith throughout the time it took to write. My mother-in-law, Carol McClymont, had the courage to remind me of the gift of life that I had received, not once, but *twice*. "Make it count, Lee Anne. You can help," she told me. My brother Drew Gibbons and sister-in-law Susan LaCivita spent countless hours on the cell phone with me. I sought Drew's opinion about the topic of fear. It was not until I heard him say, "I understand what you mean," that I would move onto another section of this book. My sister Lisa Wnuck and her husband David encouraged me to write this book and share our family's experience with cancer, career change, and relocation. It was Lisa who taught me to laugh at the predicament I had found myself in when I resigned from my career as a hospital administrator. Though it was no laughing matter to walk away from a career spanning 19 years (from 1986 to 2005), she was able to draw my attention to the lessons I had learned through it all. Thank you, Lisa.

My daughter Emma grew *along* with me as I wrote. She arrived into this new life in the Carolinas as a hopeful second grader. She taught me how to explore. She patiently sat in the backseat of the car while I became better at navigating the Triangle cities of Raleigh, Durham, and Chapel Hill. My husband Bill knew how to love me through it all and never once looked backwards. *He is the true reason we have this book.*

I also thank you, the reader, as you hold this book in your hands. Whenever one person enters into a silent agreement with himself or herself to grow stronger, the world swells in hope. I am mindful of your wish to grow, and I honor you with this book. You have taken the first step along a pathway that I believe will bring you a deeper understanding of yourself, your relationship with others, and your relationship with our Creator. Peace.

—Lee Anne McClymont
Hillsborough, NC
April 2010

Contents

Acknowledgments ix

Disclaimer xvii

Invocation xix

Preface xxi

Introduction: How I Came to Write This Book xxiii

Chapter 1: How This Book Works 1

Chapter 2: The Truth About Fear Mythology: Fears, Fables, and Falsehoods 21

Chapter 3: Reclaiming Lost Property 41

Chapter 4: Running Away: Why Beginnings and Endings Look Alike 45

Chapter 5: Fear as a Neutral Partner 49

Chapter 6: Recognizing Intuition: Staging a Rebel-ution 53

Chapter 7: Create a Happy Ending: Dreamspace Destiny Calls 57

Chapter 8: Framing Feelings in Language 63

Chapter 9: Fear Location and Collateral Recovery 69

Chapter 10: The Intention of Fear: Shining Your Fear Flashlight 73

Chapter 11: Parallel Experiences, Congruent Lessons 75

Chapter 12: Making Sense of It All: The Fear Factor 79

Chapter 13: Point of Departure 83

Appendix A: Outline of Exercises 87

Appendix B: The Fear-o-meter 91

Appendix C: Additional Resources for Further Help 93

About the Author 95

Disclaimer

Fear has the power to stop us from getting the help we need. Perhaps one of the most valuable lessons this book can give you is to help you assemble enough history with your own fear-filled experiences to recognize that you may need professional help. I encourage you to seek that help if necessary.

Friendly Fear Notebook is not a diagnostic tool. Nor is it to be used as a substitute for the advice of a seasoned mental health professional. Be sure to talk to your doctor or other healthcare provider if during the course of reading and working with this book you feel overwhelmed, discouraged, or depressed. Seek help immediately if you feel suicidal. If you need assistance finding a local mental health professional, you will find some helpful resources in the Appendix.

At this point, you may be wondering how you can use this book to support a friend or family member who struggles with fear. While it is true that many of the book's exercises will bridge understanding between you and the people in your life who struggle with fear, it is also true that you can never *completely* know or understand another person's feelings about a situation or event. Yet we all have some capacity to imagine their viewpoint. This ability is called empathy, and it's a hallmark of our humanity. I suggest you use empathy with skill.

How? *Friendly Fear Notebook* can help build a new viewpoint about fear by presenting a systematic approach to ordering the fear-filled experiences of your life. While I have directed the conversations in this book to address you, the reader, and your personal experience with fear, you may want make an association between your experience with fear and another person's struggle.

I have found that when you strengthen your own Friendly Fear skills and practice drawing from your own personal encounters with fear, you are *modeling growth and adaptation* for friends and family members. We can only support others' transformation through our own transformation. Remember the pre-flight safety review that all flight attendants recite before takeoff? Reach for your own oxygen mask before assisting someone else with his or hers.

Reading this book and journaling about your own relationship with fear offers the additional value of having first-hand experience with the exercises as your friend or family member starts out on his or her own voyage through the book. Your example will provide comfort and courage. The insights *Friendly Fear Notebook* will help you gather will in turn help you to honor the private pain and frustration that the person you want to help may be experiencing. In addition, your own experience with this book can help your friend or family member celebrate his or her own success stories.

Invocation

Healing Songwriter weave me a tale
To forget and recall
To order that which is countless
And to spin tales yet untold.

Dare to listen
Imbued with falsehood speaking truth.
I sing.
Voiceless echoes summon time and memory.

Muses
Give me the strength to begin
The forbearance to continue and
The wisdom to remember.

Lee Anne McClymont
Canton, Massachusetts
February 1986

Preface

- Have you ever found yourself confronted with a choice without knowing what to do?
- Have you ever had a deep desire to change a big part of your life, yet stall getting started?
- Have you sacrificed to make a significant change, and then returned to a former behavior time after time, finding yourself looking back in exhaustion and frustration asking, "Why did I even bother?"

If you have answered "yes" to any of these questions, this book is for you. *Friendly Fear Notebook* is your own personal primer for change. Why? Because one of the most serious roadblocks to honoring change is fear. I know this is true because of my own experience dealing with cancer, job loss, and relocation. Fear was a dominant feature in my life for many years. Stealthy? Yes. Powerful? Beyond belief.

Friendly Fear Notebook gives you the tools you need to recognize and find a passage through your fear. I call these fear-navigation skills Decision Vision. They help you learn from your past experiences with fear and teach you how to approach new fear-filled situations with greater confidence. Over the course of the 12 exercises in this book, you will create your own personal scrapbook of fear-filled moments from your life. Through guided journaling, you will practice fear-navigation skills within a safe staging area and you'll be encouraged to seek out new opportunities with a fresh perspective.

In this way, *Friendly Fear Notebook* will fuel your appetite for personal growth. Most of us who seek transformative change encounter fear as a major impediment to success. The more developed your Friendly Fear skills grow, the easier it will be for you to navigate around fear and adapt swiftly when change enters your life. In time, you will build skills that will lead you safely through fear whenever you encounter it.

Friendly Fear Notebook helps you in six simple and effective ways. This book:

1. Creates a safe place to let you look at what you are afraid of and how it has held you back.
2. Allows you to try out new approaches to solving the challenges that inevitably come with change.
3. Teaches you to unscramble what your fear is trying to tell you so that you can be *proactive* instead of *reactive*.
4. Improves decision-making skills.
5. Jump-starts conversations with family and friends about fear by teaching how to ask questions in a simple and direct way.
6. Makes imagination your key to learning playful yet effective approaches to fear.

Introduction

How I Came to Write This Book

I wrote *Friendly Fear Notebook* because of my own experience dealing with what's perhaps the ultimate fear: the fear of death. My story spans a series of life-changing events which occurred within two and half years—my mother's death from sinus cancer, my own diagnosis of stage-three non-Hodgkin's lymphoma, my departure from an employer of 15 years (and from my career itself), and my family's re-location to North Carolina from New York. I hit them all on this journey, and much to my surprise, I am still here—and now sharing my story with you as you prepare to undertake your own personal journey to build a more positive relationship with fear.

The arc of my work is based on inspiring people to create a new mindset that allows fear to coexist within us. This new approach ultimately allows fear to integrate more harmoniously into our personalities. The story that led me to this work began one hot, August night as our family was driving back to North Carolina from a vacation on Cape Cod, where we had been visiting my in-laws. My husband Bill, our nine-year-old daughter Emma, and I were in the car waiting on line for the EZ Pass tollbooth, heading south at the Tappan Zee Bridge in

New York. The EZ Pass reader was malfunctioning, so the tollbooth attendant had to get out of his station, stop traffic, and close the lane.

We were threading our way back into a "not-so-EZ Pass" toll lane when I decided to break the news to them. They sat in disbelief as I outlined my plans for my new work as a fear teacher. We were five hours into our 14-hour drive, so we had plenty of time to explore this topic, and I had a captive audience. Since I wasn't driving, Bill had to stay awake and listen to my arguments in favor of my new work and the benefits it could bring to our family and to many other families just like us.

Yet within minutes, he was on board. "You are going to talk and write about fear because you think it will help people make better decisions?" he asked.

"Yes, Bill," I answered, using my confident big-girl voice. This was the first and last conversation we ever had about the *value* of this message. Bill knew all too well the power of fear as it played out in our lives.

Though Bill and Emma were a bit startled to hear about my new career, the news did not come as a surprise to my mother-in-law, Carol. She had known something had been up during our visit. One night after supper, Carol and I had sat down together at the dining room table. I had mentioned that all week long, I had been getting up in the pre-dawn hours. In her own sassy way, Carol had asked me, "Just why are you getting up so damn early? What's that all about?"

Without thinking, I had answered: "I get up early, open up a notebook, and these words just come pouring out. But they are more than words, they're stories. I think that I am writing a play, but I can't tell."

"So how did you know to get a pen and start writing?" she had asked, intrigued.

"Well, it got to the point where I was having these conversations with myself out loud, and I realized I might wake up Bill and Emma," I had answered. "So to keep quiet, I started writing down what it was I was thinking about, and before I knew it, it was 9:30 a.m. and I had almost filled up a notebook." What I had not revealed to her at that time was that most of these conversations I wrote about had centered on my relationship with fear.

My family and I had passed through several major life changes in a very short period of time, but it was not until I began to write in my notebook on those predawn mornings on Cape Cod that I became aware of the intense emotions that accompanied me in my new life in the South. Not surprisingly, the move to North Carolina two years previously had not seemed to make any sense at all to our extended family and friends. Some people were actually hurt to learn the news of our plans to leave the city and stage a quiet retreat into the woods of North Carolina. Retreat? Only the vanquished retreat—the victor parades. Well, at least that's how I *used* to think. The very words "vanquished" and "victor" made me uneasy because I was feeling like a little of both. How could this be possible? I wondered.

During the time we were living in New York, very few people were aware that I had already undertaken my first major relocation—the relocation of my soul, by way of cancer. And how could they have known? I myself had barely begun to acknowledge the degree to which cancer had shifted my world only *after* we moved to North Carolina. I was already two years into the move before I had any clear idea about just how I was going to address the emotional upheaval brought about by disease, job loss, and physical relocation.

After that visit to Cape Cod, I recognized my need to grow through writing. I also learned how to reconcile the role writing serves in my own life as well as in the lives of the many people who would follow me on their journeys through *all* forms of loss and recovery. Documenting my journey through words was the gateway for my new life as a fear teacher.

Originally, Bill and I had approached the move to North Carolina as a scouting expedition for what we called our family's "great experiment." When we left New York City on August 1, 2005, I packed only summer clothes, leaving all of the other stuff in our apartment on 86th Street. I remember the sense of newness intensely. We signed a three-month lease for a sunny, two-bedroom, furnished apartment in Chapel Hill. Though it was a short-term lease, we knew we would spend at least one year in North Carolina to limit the disruption to Emma's school year. We had had enough emotional and physical disruption in our lives over the past year and we needed some quiet time to restore our balance. We found North Carolina to be the perfect entry into a new lifestyle that was free from city-life struggles.

Emma's school started on August 20, 2005. Within a matter of weeks, we were in a new social setting with an entirely different set of ground rules. The South remains intact when it comes to manners, I discovered. Since the rulebook is unwritten, keen observation and silence are your best teachers. We met some wonderful families from our new school who were eager to help us adapt to this new, more genteel world. In addition to their coaching, one of my closest friends from college who had spent time in southern Virginia taught me this invaluable phrase: "You might be right." I've found that it is an all-powerful tool that can diffuse any misunderstanding, and I use it deftly now, thinking of it as my "baking soda in the fridge," when conversations take awkward turns.

We had plenty of time to get familiar with the new region and to prepare Emma for her first day of school. Foolishly, I had packed her old school shoes and she didn't want new ones. For her, they had become the silent bridge between her old school, The Convent of the Sacred Heart, and her new school, St. Timothy's School of Raleigh. But Emma was growing so much that summer, and deep down I knew that by the end of August the old shoes would no longer fit. The thought of these shoes not fitting her feet freaked me out, and although I tried, I could not buy replacements down here. Even Nordstrom didn't carry them.

Then I got an idea. I decided I could stretch them, so I started to place two sweet potatoes in each shoe every night after she went to sleep. In the morning, before she woke up, I would go into her closet and slip each sweet potato out. So I resigned myself to stretching Emma's shoes at night, and metaphorically stretching myself, as well, with a sweet potato. Those tubers taught me an important lesson: whatever I brought with us into this new life I could make work. All I had to do was stretch just enough to make it fit.

You may not be surprised to hear, then, that I secretly named the journal I wrote on Cape Cod *Sweet Potatoes*. This journal became a soundboard and my truest friend—a place I could run to when I needed to grow strong. I had not opened this place to any friends until I began to adapt it for your use as *Friendly Fear Notebook*. I hope you can find within this story a connection to your own life and your own choices as well as find within yourself the strength to stretch.

During the transition between New York City and Chapel Hill, I began to call myself an "expolitan." Yes, that's right. In my journal, I made up my own word to describe the level of chaos underlying my identity struggle. Who knew? My family's roots ran deep in New England. I am a fifth-generation hometown girl from Canton, MA, who went through high school, college, and graduate school in that same state. One weekend I wore a black gown to receive my master's degree, and the very next weekend I wore a white one to marry Bill, who has been my husband for 20 years now. Since his consulting practice was based in New York City and New Jersey, we made our home in

Manhattan's Upper East Side, where I worked in a leading medical center as an administrator. Stable and happy, we lived, worked, and played in New York City for 16 years. Our roots reached deep into the Northeast, binding us to roles and lifestyles that precluded alterations. I never anticipated that a change in my professional life would lead me to relocate my family to the South, where I had ample space to consider revisions.

It was only on that Cape Cod vacation in August 2007 that I began to realize a deep need to restore my identity. Somehow, it got erased over the years, innocently blotted out by marriage, career, and motherhood. Anyone who has relocated will be familiar with these two questions: Who are you, and why are you here? For me, these questions precipitated a crisis that came to head in a friendly way. One of our new friends whose children were also in Emma's new school asked us directly if we were part of the Witness Protection Program.

We laughed—at first. Then I grew concerned and began to doubt my own judgment. Were we that conspicuous that blending in was out of the question? What exactly was it that made people so curious about our family's decision to leave Manhattan and try to make a new life in the country? Looking back, I shouldn't have been surprised. After all, we spoke openly about our thoughts on politics and religion. As New Yorkers, we ate, drank, and slept with controversy, an unlikely bedfellow for polite Southerners.

We recognized that the social landscape had indeed changed when we saw discussions stall as they turned toward touchy-feely things like why toll roads bugged us or why "Yes, ma'am" sounded like sarcasm. We discovered that in the South, one finishes his or her thoughts in conversation *before* another person speaks. Interruptions are viewed as clumsy and self-centered. (By the way, we also discovered that listening skills are sharper in the South. Rarely do you have to repeat yourself.) We may have no longer looked like urban New Yorkers—we bought clothes that were colorful and lightweight and moved anything black to the back of the closet—but we certainly remained outspoken. I felt out of step and decided to turn inward to restore balance and confront some unfinished business.

I was adrift in the newness of the South. The excitement was as intoxicating as the winter jasmine buds blooming by my front porch. Instinctively, I knew I needed some grounding before I could l reinvent myself, but I had no idea how difficult that would be. Nor did I fully comprehend what events would bring that chapter in my life to a climax. None of it made any sense *until I began to write*.

I discovered that my small-town roots from Canton lay just beneath the city-girl persona I had grown comfortable wearing. It was a quiet, hot day in my new home when I openly acknowledged to myself that my roots felt more like a starting point rather than an anchor. Roots alone would never contain the juicy essence of my identity now. The frequent journeys I made between the old apartment on 86th Street and new Carolina farmhouse, old life and new life, were nothing more than a dance between loss and recovery, memories and dreams. As each phase ushered in new growth, old labels and expectations fell away.

Besides, my roots could not compete with the vibrant new sounds, smells, and sights of the South. Here the birds sing throughout the year, all day long. The frogs' nighttime chorus often makes outdoor conversation impossible after dark. Stillness pervades as the stars dim and the sun rises. Within this wedge of time, I was shaping a new relationship with fear that would forever change the way I think.

Time wasn't waiting for me. The longer these disconnected feelings lasted, the riskier my life felt. And my family was growing restless adjusting at Sweet Wood, the name we gave to our new home. After a year of renting apartments both in Chapel Hill and North Raleigh, we had bought a house in historic Hillsborough, 37 miles northwest of Raleigh and 17 miles north of Chapel Hill. Yes, it was rural. But the choice to live on large stretch of wooded property was simple. We needed to take the lessons we learned in New York City into a new venue where we had room to grow without colliding into past expectations of each other and ourselves.

Our family's departure from Manhattan had been hastened by my resigning from my job. I had been a hospital administrator in a premier academic medical center for more than 14 years before being diagnosed with lymphoma. After nine months of chemo, punctuated by four lengthy hospitalizations, I had lost some momentum in my career. Nonetheless, I had I survived both the disease and the treatment and began planning for my return to work. I was eager to drop my "sick mommy" job title to regain my status as a full-time working mommy. As far as I could see, I was trading up.

But I was never fully welcomed back to my workplace. In fact, the day before I was to return to work, I received a letter from my boss telling me that I was fired. Shocked, I dutifully called the human resources office to process the paperwork.

"You're *fired?*" stuttered the labor relations manager, even more surprised than I was. Apparently my immediate supervisor had sent the letter without consulting human resources or the legal department. The next day, I received another phone call from human resources that went something like this: "Lee Anne, I have got some great news for you. You know that letter your boss wrote? Well, tear it up and welcome back." Talk about weird...

Apparently, labor law prohibited my employer from firing me within a year of my return-to-work date. Though I knew I wasn't welcome, now I *had* to return to work. If I chose not to go back, they could fire me for job abandonment, which would make finding another job pretty difficult. I found myself in an awkward place. Yet I was confident that my own talent and newly found sense of purpose would restore whatever momentum I had lost. At the time of my return, I did not hold anyone fully responsible for the timing of my discharge letter because I believed that management was acting emotionally. Firing me at this late stage of the process did not make sense to me, since they held my position open well beyond the mandatory limit required by labor law. In hindsight, I now see that management actually *was* surprised that I had survived this advanced stage of cancer and truly did not know what to do with me when I was announced that I was planning to return.

I construed their behavior as childish, but not lethal. I was wrong. Within three months, the situation grew untenable and hostile. But it was not until my annual performance review six months later that I knew I had made a mistake by going back. After 14 years of stellar performance evaluations, I received a review that was neutral. I knew I had to leave.

Bill and I carefully weighed all of my options. I chose to resign from my job and seek protection through the courts, filing a complaint at the Equal Employment Opportunity Commission (EEOC) for discrimination against cancer survivors. I had taken my medical leave before the HIPPA Privacy Rule took effect, and everyone knew that I had cancer. Though I had first chosen to overlook what that might do to my career, the truth was that the damage was irreversible. I filed a complaint in January 2005. By April, my case headed to arbitration and we fixed a date to appear before an arbitrator in June.

The night before the case was heard, Bill and I had a heart-to-heart conversation. Whatever the settlement offer would be, we knew that it would be a combination of some amount of money and some extension of healthcare benefits. How much, how little, or how long, we had no idea. As we discussed our options that night in our bedroom, it grew very clear to both of us that the value of my experience throughout this process would be in teaching others how to protect themselves in similar situations. It was a long and fitful night in which I was left to think about what I truly wanted from this situation. Bill knew instinctively how the negotiations would play out before the EEOC, but he had to let me churn to figure it out for myself.

The next day, I appeared in a small conference room with an EEOC arbitrator in downtown New York. After six hours, my employer came up with a final offer made under the condition that I sign a gag clause. When I asked why, I was told, "Oh, *all* settlements include this type of clause." Really? I suddenly understood why they had been so eager to settle. The ethos within the leadership ranks at the time was a pay-your-way-out-of-trouble mindset. I declined their offer. I didn't need the money. I *did* need my good name. I was blessed to have Bill urge me to walk away from the table. He was right.

Fast forward to two years after the very day my resignation took effect: I was a stay-at-home mother, living in rural North Carolina, trying to figure out just which exit I took from the freeway that brought me to this place. Was I in Cancer Survivors' Purgatory? Feelings were bubbling up, and as quickly as they would rise, I would stifle them. Blame? Neglect? Guilt? All of the above. Slowly, these emotions yielded to feelings of gratitude, recovery, and hope. My struggle was not in assigning blame, but rather in embracing the movement between loss and recovery, collapse and restoration.

In fact, over those two years, our family's entire journey traveled between the two boundaries of loss and recovery from loss. Time passed, but this pattern remained. Only in later years did I understand how this dynamic helps you grow. When you stop experiencing loss and recovery, you get stalled somewhere. If you are honest, you say to yourself, "OK. I am stuck. Now what am I supposed to do?" As soon I as I asked myself that question, I realized that a door had opened.

Would it not be easier to pack all the loss away in some imaginary box, taping it up like much of the stuff we packed from the city, and place it all in a storage tub to be lost to time and memory? I was tempted but re-considered. After all, what was the point of walking away from a job, a home, and friends without knowing why I left in the first place? Beginnings and endings look alike, and I was starting to learn just how they resonate. Unresolved feelings come along with us as we usher in new beginnings. In silence they wait, cranky for more room.

Fear is a sticky feeling. When it is not explored and diffused through writing or talking to friends and family, fear can undermine our plans and encroach upon the space we reserve for hope. Fear also co-opts our ability to trust. It makes its way alongside of us wherever we go. Since fear is ever-present, I began to realize, perhaps it may be a good idea to learn more about it and befriend it. But how? As I tried to understand my city friends' reactions to our move South, I recognized how deeply fear influenced their response to our relocation and the *silent* indictment of city life that the move implied.

Eventually, I started to understand why many of our friends viewed our relocation as "starting over." They were wrong. Well, at least partly wrong. More than getting a fresh start, we saw the move as a way to support our family's healing.

For me, that healing meant making peace with fear. I began to see writing in my journal, *Sweet Potatoes*, as the key to building a new relationship with fear—one that I could never have imagined building while living in New York City. I wrote that original journal in such a way that I could return to it again and again with fresh answers to familiar questions. I did this by writing a series of questions in the notebook, while leaving lots of blank spaces in between the questions for my answers—and in doing so, I was subconsciously giving myself the space to recall, detach, and then revisit the experience through what I'd write about it. Surprisingly, I discovered that all of my questions centered on fear and the relationship I had build with it over my life.

So now you see that I did not start writing a book to help *other* people navigate fear. No, I wrote this book to help *me* navigate fear and to create a method for teaching me how to respond to it constructively again and again. Those pre-dawn mornings on Cape Cod had cleared a pathway for me. Little did I know that this would become the foundation for the book that you are now reading, a book which might in turn clear a pathway for you, as well.

After I returned home to Sweet Wood following that Cape Cod vacation in August 2007, I continued to write about fear, but not in an abstract way. I gathered up my intense memories of the fear-filled moments in my life and placed them in neat little sentences that grew into paragraphs. I could see that I was re-living each experience as I wrote. Every time I read through them, they were making me grow. Each example gently nudged me to take responsibility for my decisions and taught me how to reconcile the emotion of fear within the whole array of human emotions. Ultimately, these little paragraphs in my journal showed me just how to integrate fear within my personality rather than try to run away from it or suppress it. I was learning acceptance at a time when all I knew was resistance.

Though many of these stories were painful to recall, they all belonged to me. They made me who I am—like a sweet potato growing underground, nurtured by the soft, rich soil warming the root, and awaiting harvest. Within months, I had developed enough material to sort and organize my story. I saw a pattern in my reactions to fear-filled situations, and that became a core element of this book. The questions that I had been asking myself out loud on Cape Cod provided me with a safe stage to assemble memory strands. From there, I was able to distill those emotions down into words. I was employing a new skill to help me move forward in my life. I was gathering a perspective from these painful experiences, finding the courage to confront the truth that created them, and then learning to exploit my own history lessons.

Over and over again, I reviewed my notes from Cape Cod. In the fall of 2007, I would drop off my fourth grader at school in Raleigh and then secretly squirrel myself away in the nearby parking lot to re-read my notes from August. Each time I read through *Sweet Potatoes*, I started to feel better and more in control of my life and the choices I had made. It was as if, over the years, the innermost part of me found a passageway out through those pages and was eagerly aligning with my outside life.

The questions that I asked myself in the notebook nurtured my sense of direction. It was through this self-interview process that I had located my own personal road map. Tucked inside as a bonus was a little bottle of Krazy Glue tagged with this message: Ready for assembly. The separation of the pieces of my life and personality had not been a psychological breakdown as much as they had been an emotional collapse. So I began to piece my life back together. It was never going to be the same life that I once had, but it was going to be a life made up from the same past experiences.

Now I know that collapse is a natural process. Without collapse, we cannot begin to restore and to rebuild. But at the time, I couldn't seem to get my arms around the notion that just about everything I knew, built, and loved was gone. Until I could learn to use fear to help me make peace with collapse and process these changes, my recovery would be stalled. Fear had been blocking my progress as doubt had taken center stage, working its way into my bones, absorbing energy and withering hope.

The voice of self-doubt shouted, "What if my remission ends?" But the most frightening question I asked myself became, "What if my family stops loving me because I brought them along with me on this messy journey?"

Fear of death, guilt, failure, and abandonment—I held it all, tucked deep inside. But the work I started with *Sweet Potatoes* led me to be curiously drawn into processing *how* I had come to understand fear and its power over my life. While I was asking questions and writing answers, I had quietly discovered that I was crafting an entry and exit strategy to the most fear-filled moments in my life. I had created a dialogue with past, present, and future and had formed a safe passageway linking all of them as I framed the exercises in this book. I could now return to each painful fear-filled event within the safety of my notebook. I could experience beginning, middle, and end and then consider new conclusions to all of these situations. In this process, I was growing stronger and more confident, and I had unwittingly improved my decision-making skills because I mastered a way to diffuse the emotional distraction that fear creates. Paralysis yielded to reason. Hope got its chance.

Lastly, no discussion about fear can take place without acknowledging the social and economic landscape I looked out upon as I wrote this book. Wall Street tumbled in the fall of 2008. Europe and Asia, caught in the world market collapse, are struggling to regain balance. Recovery is underway, but it is slow. The debt service associated with stimulus packages looms dangerously close to extinguishing the very recovery these instruments were destined to birth.

From quarter to quarter, the labor force re-aligns in ever-changing patterns. Employers shift priorities. Employees, insecure, contract with fear. Relationships, whose sole purpose is to protect and preserve, break under stress.

Given this social context, the following three questions arose in my mind as I considered adapting *Sweet Potatoes* into *Friendly Fear Notebook*:

- How will you remember this period of your life?
- Has fear's influence changed during this time?
- Where can you turn to organize *your* story of loss *and* recovery?

In the following pages, you'll learn just how valuable an ally fear can be.

Chapter 1
How This Book Works

View the time you spend in this chapter as an orientation period to a whole new way of thinking about fear and the role it plays in your life. You may be tempted to skip ahead and go straight to the exercises, but I warn you: Don't overlook the advantages good preparation brings to this process and to your success in building your own personal narrative.

I'd like to start by giving you an overview of each chapter, describing what lies ahead on your journey through *Friendly Fear Notebook*. The rest of this chapter will feature some overall strategies and helpful hints for how to approach this work that will set you up for success. I'll speak to you candidly about the time and sweat equity you will need to write your own *Friendly Fear Notebook*, and I'll address the subject of setting expectations.

The end of this chapter introduces you to the concept of Tool School, a collection of devices designed to jumpstart you on your journey. Here, you will meet the first two Tool School topics, **The Fear-o-meter** and **Sight Setting,** which will help you see where you stand with fear right now and where you want to end up after reading this book.

Chapter 2, *The Truth About Fear Mythology: Fears, Fables, and Falsehoods*, breaks down the entire book into small pieces. I think of it as a bite-size presentation of the entire book. I did this expressly to avoid any risk you may have of feeling overwhelmed at any one point of this process of exploring Friendly Fear.

At the start of Chapter 2, I'll share with you how I altered inherited fables about how fear works and learned how to limit fear to the roles of effective coach and navigator. This chapter will help you destroy your preconceived notions about fear so you can make room to write a new story about how you view fear. In doing this, you will use a new skill called Decision Vision, which offers you the opportunity to look at a fear-filled situation from an entirely different perspective.

Chapter 2 ends with more Tool School topics, including the Privacy Contract, My Friendly Fear Notebook's Title Page, The Flip Side, and Fear Vortex.

As you work through *Friendly Fear Notebook*, you will be creating an intimate portrait of the emotional journey of your life. As an emotional gesture of respect for that intimacy, I will ask you to sign and date a **Privacy Contract**—a personal contract for you to make with yourself to remind you to honor your experiences and the privacy they'll need to both teach and heal. I've found this to be invaluable in my workshops.

My Friendly Fear Notebook's Title Page allows you to create a title for your own *Friendly Fear Notebook*. (I still use the name *Sweet Potatoes* for mine.) When you name your own *Friendly Fear Notebook*, you impart your own signature to its contents and endow it with the powerful reflection of your own, inimitable self.

The Flip Side is your first opportunity in the book to play with Decision Vision. Here, I'll ask you to take your first baby steps in changing your mind about fear, just in time to dive into the final Tool School topic, **Fear Vortex,** which is also the first formal exercise of the book. This is a chart that provides you with a safe space to deconstruct a fearful situation, helping you separate fact from fiction. It's an excellent launching pad into the exercises in the chapters that follow.

> ### Friendly Fear Approaches
>
> The exercises in this book use three different approaches, each with its own objective:
> * Assessment, where you will write about your past fear experiences and describe the impact these experiences have upon your current quality of life
> * Detachment, where you'll sever the connection between past, present, and future, which is necessary for developing strong fear-navigation skills
> * Design, where you will use the power of imagination to build new responses to experiences that you have found to be fear-filled in the past
>
> In some cases, these approaches will be explicit directions, while in other cases, they will be presented more subtly. Either way, they work to move you gently toward assembling a personal narrative with fear. They also provide a safe and secure staging area for you to learn and to practice new responses to fear that serve to forward your goals and objectives, not thwart them.

Chapter 3, *Reclaiming Lost Property*, reminds you of the benefit of building your Friendly Fear skills. Here you begin to gather specific and perhaps painful, fear-filled moments in your life and then describe these events in writing. You may find sketching a memory helps reveal a uniform pattern to this experience. Although I am more comfortable using words than pictures, some of you will prefer to draw your memories. You may wish to sketch your way through *Friendly Fear Notebook*. If you do, I strongly suggest that you include titles to your sketches so that in the future, you can return to these pages and easily recall the exact moment in your personal fear narrative that each sketch depicts. Titles may prevent any ambiguity that could set in over time, blurring the lines between one specific fear-filled experience and a general abstraction of fear that would be less helpful for this project.

Chapter 4, *Running Away: Why Beginnings and Endings Look Alike*, gently navigates you beyond detachment. In this chapter you are asked to describe times that you remember running away. Until you learn to confront the truth about a situation and the fear it provokes, you will never be able to accept it, find the courage to interrupt it, and move beyond it. This is why for many of us, beginnings and endings look alike.

Chapter 5, *Fear as a Neutral Partner*, is a playful chapter written to give you a break from all your hard work so far. The exercise in this chapter asks you to consider times when you were successful at moving beyond fear to neutralize its impact on your behavior. The exercise organizes your memories so that you learn to recognize the common ground shared between your successful experiences with fear.

At this point, you are ready to adopt a fresh approach to fear that synthesizes the lessons you already know. Now you can begin to replace less effective reactive strategies with more effective pro-active behaviors. Knowing how to anticipate your own feelings when confronted with a past fear-filled event, you are asked to design a new response that places you back in control of the situation, thus re-claiming your confidence.

Chapter 6, *Recognizing Intuition: Staging a Rebel-ution*, marks a clear departure from recollection and takes you into revision. The exercises presented in this section ask you to think about the ways that fear has reduced your powers to build a strong relationship with yourself and also with your friends and family. How does fear manage to do this? Fear co-opts our ability to trust. This ability to trust forms the contours of *all* relationships that we build with others and ourselves. In addition to learning how to trust our relationships with other people, we also must learn how trust our own talents and experiences. This special form of trust is called intuition.

Chapter 7, *Create a Happy Ending: Dreamspace Destiny Calls*, returns you to the driver's seat, but it asks that you leave your analytical brain in the garage. For many people, memorization and the accumulation of facts embody learning and education. The truth is that as valuable as those skills are, none can replace imagination.

Imagination is a form of intellect that we use to craft our vision of the world we live in. Without this gift, our vision flattens and all the analytical powers of the world cannot hoist us above the everyday fray. Only imagination can help us build hope and trust.

Chapter 8, *Framing Feelings in Language*, teaches you how to organize your fear vocabulary and then sort through the impact these words have on your feelings. For many readers, this is their favorite chapter because it strikes at the heart of all of fear-filled experiences. What we think has the power to influence our minds and thus, our behavior. Once we write down those thoughts in words and take a good look at them, their power fades. After this chapter, you may feel the ground shift as you call into question closely held beliefs about yourself and witness them undergo a dramatic revision.

Chapter 9, *Fear Location and Collateral Recovery*, shows you how to build your own timeline. At this point, you may be asking, "Where does the repo man fit in here?" In the rush to avoid painful memories, we sometimes store these experiences in places they don't belong. Feelings bubble up, and in the interest of time, we stuff those feelings back into our heart, ignoring the warning they bring us. In some extreme cases we ransom our own health to support a denial mechanism hungry for space and emotional energy. This chapter asks a simple question: Where does your fear live? As soon as you *discover* its favorite hiding place, you will be able to *re-cover* the space that it has consumed in your life.

Chapter 10, *The Intention of Fear: Shining Your Fear Flashlight*, probes the connection we unconsciously make between fear and intention. Up until this point, the chapters in the book have been built on examining your experiences with fear. From here on, the chapters will invite you to honestly assess your own role in contributing to fear's strength and power over your own life. Your Fear Flashlight is particularly powerful because it challenges you to set the record straight by confronting your fears in the comfort and safety of the perspective of time.

Chapter 11, *Parallel Experiences, Congruent Lessons,* organizes another memory strand. In this chapter, you compare and contrast the feelings of falling in love with the feelings of falling in fear. This may seem like a strange association, but the point is to help you see with fresh eyes the beauty and promise that are often held in fear-filled situations. Instead of trying to avoid fear-filled situations altogether, you learn here to use your experience to guide you through these situations and honor the growth they promise.

Chapter 12, *Making Sense of It All: The Fear Factor,* is the culmination of all the previous chapters. This chapter shows you how to divest the emotional distraction that fuels fear. As you have created your own *Friendly Fear Notebook,* you may now begin *to shift your emphasis away from ignoring fear to befriending fear.* Harness the energy fear brings into any situation, and listen to what fear is trying to tell you about yourself. Practice you new approach in the safety of your own notebook and revise your own experience with fear-filled events.

Chapter 13, *Point of Departure,* celebrates the accomplishment of writing your own *Friendly Fear Notebook* and opens the doorway to a deeper understanding of hope and faith no longer obstructed by fear.

In the back of the book, the *Appendix* includes an outline of the exercises, another copy of **The Fear-o-meter,** and a listing of additional resources for further help.

By the way, I've adapted some of the material in *Friendly Fear Notebook* from the "Harness Fear, Harvest Hope" workshops that I gave in Hamlet, NC, in the fall of 2009. I had read in our Raleigh newspaper, the *News & Observer*, that tiny Hamlet (population of 5,800) had been devastated by the recent deployment to Iraq of 76 members of Hamlet's own E Company, 120th Combined Arms Battalion, 30th Heavy Brigade Combat Team in April 2009, and I wanted to help. My intention was to share my private experience with fear to help restore hope within the community. Within four hours, I had recruited the help of the librarian and organized two workshops on consecutive weekends at the Hamlet Public Library. The participants at the workshops were courageous men and women eager to reshape their relationship with fear, and these workshops help me solidify the process I now present here.

Hints for Success

Get supplied. You'll need a pen and possibly a blank notebook or journal. You can either chose to write the answers in this book or write them in a separate notebook, so you can return to do the exercises again at a later date. As you fill the pages of your notebook, you may need to buy another one. Make sure you have the space you need to write as much as you want.

Try to do the exercises in order, but read them all before you start any. The order of the exercises is deliberate, but because they gently grow more difficult as they progress, the underlying advantage in doing the exercises sequentially may not be obvious from the start. But rest assured that each exercise provides a lesson that serves as a stepping-stone for the next group of exercises. To see this for yourself, before you begin the first exercise, turn to the Appendix at the back of this book and read the outline of all 12 exercises. That way, you'll understand where the exercises are leading and you'll trust that there is one coherent plan behind them.

Though I do hope you will stick to the order I have selected, there is no inherent danger in skipping ahead and responding to the questions that shout out to you for an immediate response. Likewise, if you find that one of the exercises stumps you, then move on to the next one with the understanding that you can return to it later after you have had some time to think.

Be flexible and stay organized. The momentum you build through the course of the book can carry you to its conclusion. Seize the momentum created in this process and let it work for you. You may find that you pass through all of these exercises swiftly, only to return to the book weeks later to begin again. None of this material comes with expiration dates. Your skills at building story and exploiting your own personal history will grow with practice.

Invite a friend next time. After you have made it through *the whole book*, think about taking a friend along with you on your second trip. Let me explain how this works. Once you build and practice your own Friendly Fear skills in private, consider opening a conversation with a family member or friend about your favorite parts of the book.

> When you invite someone into a conversation about fear, you are inviting him or her to play a larger role in your life. Sounds risky? You bet, but consider this: When we practice vulnerability, we grow more trusting and trustworthy. You may be able to help your friend sort through difficult experiences, and in the process, learn from his or her journey. Note: Your **Privacy Contract** has an escape clause that allows for this type of collaboration.

Taking Time Outs

In strategic places throughout this book, you'll see this simple suggestion: **Let's step out of the kitchen for a moment.** This translates as, "May be too heavy to lift," "You may need some privacy here," Or "Let's keep this between you, me, and this pen." Think of using this expression as wearing work gloves while you probe and examine your feelings—it's a boundary keeper that will prevent you from getting hurt as you work. Learn to use it as you talk with family and friends about the work you are doing with *Friendly Fear Notebook*. This is important work you are undertaking. Be patient with yourself and demand patience from all on-lookers.

Climate Control: "Green Space Ghetto" and "Subway Sahara"

As you prepare to work in *Friendly Fear Notebook*, please consider your own climate control. The climate I am referring to is the noise both inside and outside your head. Journaling is a sorting process. This book helps you organize a personal narrative and introduces the three techniques mentioned earlier in this chapter—assessment, detachment, and design—that can help you construct a healthier relationship with fear. All of these skills require concentration and privacy. This is especially critical when you are working through the exercises for the first time.

Undoubtedly, you will experience times of intense emotion as you explore and examine the fear-filled moments in your life. Although I do make use of the **Let's step out of the kitchen for a moment** suggestion, I cannot fully prepare you for the emotional impact that some of these questions may provoke. (Even now, as I write this chapter, I am still spinning from my own responses to Chapter 5.) Consequently, consider where you are physically and emotionally located when you approach this work, and remember that the exercises grow in difficulty as you advance. With that in mind, I will share with you now some suggestions to help you prepare the space you will need to get the job done.

During the 16 years that I lived in New York City, I sought daily refuge in Central Park. I soon learned to call it my "Green Space Ghetto." Although I may have been confined within the concrete and glass of the cityscape, I could always find in Central Park some connection to nature—grass, trees, and wide-open swatches of sky. This space restored my emotional balance. I found my thoughts could wander more freely while I as there, and this feeling of freedom stayed with me long after I left the park. Nature reminded me of my place within time and space. It anchored me to infinity and, paradoxically, helped me focus on the immediate tasks at hand.

Consider taking a stroll in your favorite park to find your own "Green Space Ghetto" as you think about your responses to these exercises. It may clear a channel to reveal an unheeded emotion or release some other insight.

Other venues exist to help you through this discovery process. Some are less obvious than others. While living in New York, I found that I could experience peace and solitude in, of all places, the #6 Express Train. This is a subway line that travels from way up north in the Bronx all the way down to the Lower East Side of Manhattan, making only express stops at select stations.

Sound like an improbable sanctuary? Yes, but I figured out that the space between the stops was just enough time for me to develop contained thoughts and hold abbreviated conversations within the quiet of my own head. The travel time between the stop at 86th Street and the stop at 68th Street became my "Subway Sahara." It gave me just enough time to block out all of the background noise in my head and focus my attention on a specific task. I miss this aspect of my life in New York City in my daily drive to Raleigh from where I now live in Hillsborough. For those of you who can relax while commuting to work or school, you have a superb opportunity to digest this work. How I hope you can see that!

My whole point here is this: Try not to get hung up on the notion of where you are when you begin this work. Instead, focus on the places and times of day when you are less likely to get interrupted and when you can anticipate a set amount of time to work on the exercises.

If you are like most people, you will need additional time as you reach the final chapters of this book. Your commitment to your progress will emerge as you make plans to find the time and space to complete your work on *Friendly Fear Notebook*.

Location, Location, Location: "Harmony Hangouts"

Take time now to consolidate your knowledge about the physical location where you will work on this project. I call these places "Harmony Hangouts," and I include some ideas below on how to identify them, create them, and get to them. If you pause here to anticipate your needs, you are more likely to be successful in your efforts with this book.

We schedule our lives around work, school drop off, the gym, and other activities. To get the most value out of the exercises in *Friendly Fear Notebook*, you will need to find a safe and secure physical space to do this work. You must be able to honor your need for time alone inside your "Harmony Hangout." For some, this may take the form of the cab of your pick-up truck, a quiet corner inside your favorite coffee shop, or your office space in off-hours. Wherever your "Harmony Hangout" is, use it to honor the time and space you will need for this work.

There are three factors to establishing a "Harmony Hangout." You must identify them, create them, and be able to visit them whenever you need to. First, try to identify an optimum space for your "Harmony Hangout." Perhaps the most vital aspect to this space is privacy. Ideally, the location you chose to work on your fear-navigation skills will have a door that you can close. The space should also be relatively quiet.

You may need to alter the space slightly to create a suitable work environment. Does the space have a comfortable chair and writing station? A comfortable ambient temperature? Sufficient lighting? If you can, consider the value of having natural lighting in your work space. Can you see the sky and watch the stars at night? Keep working on the space until it feels perfect, because hopefully, you will return to this special place long after your have finished your journey through *Friendly Fear Notebook*.

The single-most challenging aspect to your "Harmony Hangout" is actually getting to it. Give yourself permission to go there *whenever* you need to. Be considerate of your family and friends by telling them about this space and how you plan to use it. This way, they will know how to respond to your temporary separation and honor your need for privacy. Make a "Private: Keep Out, Please!" sign if you must. And don't forget to say thank you. Courtesy helps others acknowledge your private boundaries.

Actual Results May Vary

How fast you advance through this book is completely up to you. After working with many people who are doing these exercises, I have come to approach the process of Friendly Fear gently and gradually. Why? Freedoms are incrementally gained and lost. *Friendly Fear Notebook* re-establishes personal freedom by stretching horizons and reclaiming lost hope. My Southern friends here in North Carolina taught me an expression that I think is appropriate here: Always remember, real change comes real slow.

None of this work is easy. Yes, I have tried to include some playful aspects in the book, but don't let the playfulness of some of the exercises fool you. The material you are going to assemble, organize, and revise is likely to hold a significant traction within your life. Letting go of your past relationship with fear is difficult for many. ***As you write your replies to the questions* Friendly Fear Notebook *asks, be ruthless in seeking the truth behind your fears, yet be gentle in your surrender to this knowledge.***

Now it's time for Tool School. Before beginning any quest of self-discovery such as the one you are about to embark upon, it's always good to have a solid idea of where your starting point is. That way, you can better appreciate how far you've come later on. That's what **The Fear-o-meter** is all about. And immediately following that, you'll find the second Tool School topic, **Sight Setting**. Let's get started!

Tool School Topic: The Fear-o-meter

This self-assessment tool can help you recognize your current feelings about fear. There are no right or wrong answers, and you won't be scored, so just answer as honestly as you can.

On a scale from 1 to 5, please circle your responses below according to the following guidelines:

        1 = strongly agree

        2 = somewhat agree

        3 = neutral

        4 = somewhat disagree

        5 = strongly disagree

1. Fear is something I *rarely* talk about with friends or family.

        1   2   3   4   5

2. Journaling promotes self-awareness.

        1   2   3   4   5

3. I don't know how or where to begin when it comes to talking about fear.

        1   2   3   4   5

4. I would find it helpful if I had a method to help me talk about fear with my family, friends, and business associates.

        1   2   3   4   5

5. I would be willing to spend time and money to improve my fear-navigation skills.

1   2   3   4   5

As you work through this book, you may wish to look back at your initial responses here and consider how you have changed and updated your fear experiences. You will find another copy of **The Fear-o-meter** in the Appendix that you can use later for comparison.

Tool School Topic: Sight Setting

Now that you've seen your starting point, I'd like you to visualize where it is you'd like to go. I always begin my "Harness Fear, Harvest Hope" workshops by asking the participants to think about how they hope that the fear-navigation skills they're about to learn can help them. In the space below, articulate three specific objectives you have for learning about Friendly Fear.

I hope this book helps me to:

1. _____
2. _____
3. _____

If you have had trouble charting your three major objectives, you can always return to this question later.

Friendly Fear Notebook has been brought to you thanks to our sponsor, *Hope.*

Finally, before you begin *Friendly Fear Notebook*, I would like a word with you about hope. Specifically, I want to discuss how hope influences the quality of your life. As you learn to harness fear, you begin to harvest hope. Hope is a positive motivator. Hope streamlines your thinking and focuses your efforts with clarity. When you have hope, you strive. When you have hope, you grow. When you have hope, you take risks. Sometimes, hope is completely irrational, and sometimes it is 100 percent pure reason.

In other words, hope is bigger than our analytical brains. It embraces some form of intuition. For some of us, hope includes a keen sense of faith and greater purpose. However you feel toward it, hope influences the quality of your life. Consequently, hope needs space to live inside all of us.

Some of you may be at a point in life where fear has become so powerful an influence over your everyday thoughts that you have very little room to give to hope. If that's true for you, it's urgent that you grab a pen and work through *Friendly Fear Notebook*. This book will help you find hope again. It will teach you how to build a life so that you can find and preserve the space that hope needs to flourish. Of all the gifts *Friendly Fear Notebook* has to bring you, this is the greatest benefit—how to use fear to find hope.

Chapter 2

The Truth About Fear Mythology: Fears, Fables, and Falsehoods

Fear can bring power into your life, and at the same time fear can take power away. Let's look at *how* fear diminishes our own power.

Fear stops dialogue.

Fear stops love.

Fear stops change.

I know this to be true in my own life because I may own the world's largest private collection of self-help books. I bought many of these books when I first moved to North Carolina from New York City in 2005. I was in transition and trying to feel my way through the confusion. Since I know I learn from books, whenever I buy a new one, I plug into a fresh source of energy. I was on a mission to find the answer to unlocking my gears written in some book by someone else who went through this process.

Well, I never found that one book. *It doesn't exist.* The closest I ever got to finding a book with *all* the answers that I needed to help me live was the journal I started on vacation in Cape Cod in 2007—the one I named *Sweet Potatoes* and my entry point into finding Friendly Fear.

This is how I have come to suggest using self-help books: Read as many as you can to assemble a composite of the material that helped you most. And in addition to reading, start writing. Soon, you will develop the communication skills necessary to describe your feelings in words, and the benefits are tremendous.

Be prepared for one of the most rigorous interviews you will ever have in your life as you make your way through *Friendly Fear Notebook*. The truth you uncover in responding to the questions in this book will form the basis for a deeper understanding of yourself and, specifically, your own history with fear. This new genre that I've named "self-story" holds limitless potential for learning and self-enrichment. The techniques employed let you craft a vehicle and voyage safely into the difficult realm of your feelings. This has taught me to "seek the answer within," using a flexible and organized structure that keeps me focused.

Consider *Friendly Fear Notebook* as your "feelings organizer" and a safe storage place to build a composite of your working knowledge of yourself. Use the lessons drawn through other self-help books that influenced the way you see a problem or challenge. If you are like me, all of these books provided insight, but none gave complete answers. Let me give you an example.

As I was orienting to my new life in North Carolina, I drew inspiration from the book *Who Moved My Cheese* by Spencer Johnson, M.D. That was when I had my "a-ha" moment. But it did not play out the way I would have guessed. It was the final straw in my proverbial camel's back. I was driving on the I-540 interchange around I-40 in

Raleigh. Alone in the car, I suddenly started speaking out loud to myself, saying, "Lee Anne, this has got to stop. You have to move on. No more reading. You simply have to figure a way out of this mess and get moving again."

I realized in that moment that no matter how many self-help books I had read, or how many self-help DVDs I had rented, I was continuing to get stuck somewhere between knowing what to do and finding the courage to do it. This is a bad place to be. I found myself caught in the space between loss and recovery. It was dark in there. I felt alone. Although I wrote a poem about this experience, I was not yet able to process the information I knew innately as an artist in a way that made sense to me. It would take more than a poem to help me unscramble my feelings—it was going to take a whole new approach to learn about fear and how to organize those lessons in a sensible way. Writing is central to upending fear's control.

A Study of Fear Mythology

Before I named this book *Friendly Fear Notebook*, I asked myself two questions: "What is it that you know about fear, and how do you talk about it?" Not much, came the answer. I remembered a few hymns about it. The Bible talks about fear. The word "fear" appears 365 times in the King James Version—enough for one mention every day of the year. Coincidence? Uncanny. Homer, Sophocles, and Virgil speak about fear, too. Nevertheless, I could not recall reading *anything* specific about integrating fear into my daily life. Eventually, I began to explore conventional legends to figure out more about fear, and I discovered that I had inherited a fear mythology whose story line reads something like this:

> *Hero confronts fear, dressed up as a dragon.*
> *Hero slays dragon to triumph over crisis.*

My hero stories usually have a happy ending. My own personal image of fear is one that was handed down to me over the years as something that we must confront, overcome, and kill before we can triumph. But at age 45, I admitted to myself that I had outgrown this fear-slayer story line. My own emotional literacy made me skeptical. The notion was knocked on its head after I had "battled" cancer. If I had fought cancer and presumably won, then why did I have this nagging fear of recurrence? I aspired to identify my feelings and use the energy they bring to help me move forward. So I created a new kind of fear mythology for the 21st century whose headline reads:

> *Reformed dragon-slayer tames fear*

Let me review some observations about fear as it exists in modern-day America. First, conversations between family and friends about fear are scant, and finding practical steps toward integrating fear within our selves is difficult at best. We have not had in our culture a clearly defined pathway for building a positive relationship with fear. Until now.

Platitudes abound:

Look within.

We are standing on a whale fishing for minnows.

The only thing we have to fear is fear itself.

All are true. But none give instructions.

Next, the strongest take-away message I received regarding fear is that you should avoid discussing fear at all costs. Talk about instant prickliness! Conversations spasm at the slightest scent of fear, often provoking people to retreat altogether into the quiet of their own heads or hide behind a nervous giggle.

Finally, the unspoken message I received about fear is this: If you really need to get something done, close you eyes and plow ahead. Ignore fear. Avoid it. Keep on running. Say "no" to fear.

Guess what? That actually works some of the time. Try hard to ignore your fear, and indeed you may occasionally succeed. As long as you're willing to run with your eyes closed and ignore fear, you tell yourself, you'll be fine. But how many times have you, like me, been so afraid that you closed you eyes and came to a complete halt?

"I can't go any farther here because I am afraid," we say to ourselves. So we stall out. Sometimes we actually turn around and go backwards. "Not today. Maybe tomorrow. But definitely not now," we tell ourselves. Do you remember the mention in the previous section about losing hard-won gains? This is where it all starts falling apart.

What about those times when you don't have the luxury of seeking a postponement? Health crises are classic examples of this type of fear-filled situation. Major life changes like job loss, death of a loved one, or divorce also bring these concerns front and center, where fear unmanaged contributes to a growing sense of unhappiness or isolation. In each of these situations, you can't use time to hide anymore. Given this context, I have come to understand time as avoidance medicine. It works, but only for a while. And it is very, very expensive.

Let's step out of the kitchen for a moment.

Now let's examine how fear recruits avoidance to help sabotage you and how fear organizes the strength it needs to destroy opportunity and crush hope. For the next exercise, consider this hypothetical situation where you learn about the relationship between fear, avoidance, and pain. Does it sound familiar? Check in with the fear dragon mythology as a refresher.

Imagine that you have avoided something because you sensed fear. The situation has now developed into a full-blown crisis and it's taking you with it, ready or not. Delay or no delay, the fear factor (fear + avoidance) has out-maneuvered you, and you are going down.

Now let's back up and look at what just happened:

- You avoided fear by closing your eyes and ignoring it.
- Since you closed your eyes, you could no longer run.
- Consequently, you stopped...and remained standing still.

Through clever and adroit use of time, you delay some painful outcome until at last, the crisis grows so big and out of control that your own fear has conspired against you. It betrays you, and you are stuck—powerless, frozen, and sadly, victimized.

Many of us have come to this unspoken understanding. Avoidance makes fear grow. And fear has another partner called pain. Fear is pain's advance party. You smell fear before you feel the pain. It's the warning signal, the alarm that goes off in your head. It's the glimpse of the needle before the pain of the jab. Should I continue? You get the point.

We are all conditioned to connect fear with pain. As a consequence, some of us have learned to avoid fear and pain *at all costs*. We confuse avoidance with safety and kaboom!—we fall and begin to think that it is perhaps best not to get back up on our feet again. Hope gets crushed in the collision.

> **Insider's Secret:**
> **When you hear this message:**
> **"Avoid pain and fear at all costs,"**
> Stop and think. *This is a set up.*
> **SLOW DOWN**

Now that we have summarized some observations about fear, it's time again for Tool School. Read and sign the following **Privacy Contract**, and then consider giving your Friendly Fear journal a name that you can write down on **My Friendly Fear Notebook's Title Page**. A word about naming your journal (inspired by an editor who gave me a good tip about naming books): Try to come up with at least two or three possible titles for your story. You may be surprised what you discover while you do this. I know I was! Then, you'll be ready for **The Flip Side**.

Tool School Topic: Privacy Contract

Please read before you start the exercises that follow

I understand that my task is to assemble an organized approach to fear that works like a scrapbook. This scrapbook has dual powers. First, it will help me organize my past experiences with fear. Then, it will help me reduce them to their simplest terms so I can identify the common denominators and start on my journey toward effective fear navigation.

I agree to take my time. I understand that I may feel uncomfortable at some points, but I also realize that this feeling will pass as I advance through the work. My journal is private territory, and I agree to respect both my own privacy and the privacy of those I choose to work with.

By signing this contract in the space below, I am agreeing to abide by its terms.

Signature: _____

Date: _____

Tool School Topic:
My Friendly Fear Notebook's Title Page

The name of my Friendly Fear Notebook is:

_____

by

_____

(your name)

Other potential titles:

_____

_____

_____

_____

Tool School Topic: The Flip Side

This tool shows you how to use your imagination to create a three-dimensional image of your experience with fear. To start this process, ask yourself one simple question: How is fear useful?

Let me make a few suggestions as you consider your answer:
* Fear improves our awareness and alerts us to trouble.
* Fear protects us from danger.
* Fear teaches us patience.
* Fear connects us with other people.
* Fear turns our focus inward (possibly the greatest gift of all).

Can you list more good things that fear does?

_____
_____
_____
_____

Perhaps by now you have already begun to see the gifts fear has to offer.

Can you recall the fear mythology updated for the 21st century that you read about earlier in this chapter? Think about the old story line, "Hero slays dragon and triumphs," and remember how it changes into "Reformed dragon slayer tames fear." *Reformed?* Yes, you read it correctly. Here is it again: *Reformed dragon slayer tames fear.*

Imagine what could happen if you don't slay this dragon but instead figure out how to use it to help you do your work? Where would you begin to re-shape your story with fear mythology? And if a tame fear dragon does indeed exist, where would you have to travel to find him?

We will need to create a new fear mythology to get some answers. Read on and see how you may want to revise the story line.

My new fear mythology looks like this:

I learned of a tame dragon named Friendly Fear Dragon who lives in the Great Land of Transition. I decide to visit him. It happened that my timing was great because I found him playing a skillful game of Decision-Making. Decision-Making is the Friendly Fear Dragon's favorite sport. His teammates, Avoidance and Pain, are seasoned professionals supporting the Friendly Fear Dragon's game, and they help him win—most of the time.

How does this story work into your current world and the current relationship that you may have with fear? Do you recognize the Great Land of Transition within your personal borders? Here is a hint: The hallmark of a nation, state, town, family, person, or even of the *part* of a person in transition is *the fast and continuous process of decision-making.*

I hope you consider the point of this dragon tale. I shared this story to illustrate the value your imagination has over your current perception of fear. My hope is that you were able to recognize within this make-believe story some patterns—patterns that reflect aspects of your own relationship with fear and how your understanding of fear influences your own decision-making skills. I also hope that you could identity another relationship between fear, avoidance, and pain and see how they conspire to work against you in times of rapid change.

Over time, I had grown comfortable confusing safety with avoidance, and sadly, I encountered pain as a consequence. After I wrote this dragon tale, I was able to gain the perspective I desperately needed to interrupt a dangerous cycle I had innocently fallen into: *Avoid pain at all costs.*

After you have assembled your experiences in an organized way, you are capable of connecting the dots between them, and working backwards, you can decipher their context from the decisions you have made. With a little practice, a pattern will emerge from your stories of fear-filled events, and through this process your own personal playbook with fear will reveal itself.

From this point on, you can determine which approaches to fear work for you and which ones need revision. This conscious choice to see and respond to fear in a new way is a powerful skill that I call Decision Vision. It allows you to shift your focus so that you will be able to see other ideas and options that may not have occurred to you before. You end up feeling less like a victim because Decision Vision puts you back in the driver's seat. So fasten your seat belt!

As you progress through the exercises and begin to strengthen your Decision Vision, you may wish to return to the dragon tale and your own Friendly Fear Dragon in the Great Land of Transition. Ask him to play a game of Decision-Making with you. Can you imagine the satisfaction of beating the Friendly Fear Dragon at his own game? Delicious.

As you stand on the threshold of your voyage, I want to leave you with one more thought. You need to *feel* brave before you can *act* bravely. Before you start working, say this word out loud: **Scared.** You may want to say that word several times. Change the inflection of your voice. Say it fast or slow. Say it loudly or softly. The point is to acknowledge with your own voice the feeling associated with fear.

Now say this word: **Sacred.** Same letters, same sounds—but vastly different meaning and intent. As soon as you say this word out loud, you shift your emphasis away from the fear and toward another, more powerful influence. For some readers, saying this word may be shaping a one-syllable prayer to our Creator. For others, saying this word invokes the power of the universe awakening to guide your footsteps and fulfill a destiny. Wherever you may be in your journey in faith and understanding, use this technique to diffuse the intensity of the moment and invite calm back into the space.

You are now in transition between two parallel yet distinct worlds. You've come from one world that describes an inherited fear mythology and suggests a possible revision to that legend. The world you are entering is the world you are designing as your write about fear in your notebook. As you begin to do this, the new mythology of fear I created for you works quietly behind the scenes to help you avoid the pitfalls of conventional thinking.

On another level, you are leaving the land of make-believe and stepping into your own powers. This truly is *sacred space*. It is where you store your secret powers. No other human has had, has now, or will ever have the same set of talents and experience. Respect them and honor them. Consign fear to a lesser role in your own life story and see the beauty unfold.

Let's step out of the kitchen for a moment.

At this point, you are learning how to break apart the fear/pain connection. When we look into our past experiences with fear and pain, sometimes we bring the hurt along with us into the present and then carry it into the future. Unfortunately, the painful emotions of hurt and disappointment usually overshadow the lessons the experience teaches.

In many ways, when we walk into the present state with these painful memories, it's as if we picked up the wrong luggage. We meant to bring our suitcase, but in our rush to make a quick get-away, we accidentally grabbed the rubbish instead—and by the time we realize it, it's often too late. We brought the rubbish with us and left the lesson-luggage behind. There is a lot of truth to this analogy.

The stronger you become at identifying aspects of your past behavior, the easier it will be to acquire new skills that will influence new behavior. In other words, when you are confronted in the future with new challenges that bring fear with them, you will already have had experiences and lessons from your past (with your notebook) to help you navigate the fear. You will be able to give yourself ample room to study it and then recognize the power it has to either help you to grow or force you to shrink.

The best way to start learning how to do this is with a simple chart called **Fear Vortex** that I designed to help sort fear-filled events. This is both an element of Tool School and also the first of the 12 exercises in this book.

If you recall, in the first chapter, you read that hope needs space to survive. Understanding space and how to use it for your optimum benefit is part of the lessons of *Friendly Fear Notebook*, but it also shows up in skillful games of decision-making. The **Fear Vortex** asks you to chart a fear-filled experience within the space of four quadrants. In order to do this, you must consider your experience through two distinct perspectives.

First, you need to learn how to discern *necessary* fear from *unnecessary* fear (also known as worry). Next, you have to be able to tell the difference between the aspects of the fear-filled event you're charting that you *cannot* change and those aspects that you *can* change. This can be difficult at first, so I'll give you some examples before I ask you tackle it alone.

In many cases, what you classify as necessary fear one day will shift to unnecessary fear the next. This device is not meant to be a label maker. It is a safe place for you to figure out what your perception is right *now* of an event (whether it's in the past, present, or future). The lesson here is to practice consigning your fear-filled moments to a small space. This helps re-establish your control over any given situation, and you may realize that you have more control over a circumstance than you think. Use this device to brainstorm some possibilities and to practice breaking fact apart from fiction. Send fear a warning. It's about to run out of real-estate.

As we all know, history often has a predictive nature. With a little practice and imagination, you should be able to predict you own behavior in future situations. Once you learn how to use the **Fear Vortex** fluently, play with it. Turn it around and see if you can figure out how a person you are relating to may feel about the fear-filled situation he or she is confronting. Don't worry about getting the wrong answers there. The exercise isn't about getting it all right. It's about encouraging you to walk in the other person's shoes for a moment to see how this person might be caught in his or her own vortex of fear.

Parents, pay attention! Adult children caring for aging parents, listen up! Managers, open your ears! Community leaders, tune in! Fear triggers abound when the individuals around you feel less control over their decisions. The **Fear Vortex** can help you assess a situation quickly and respond to your needs by anticipating fear-filled experiences. Try talking about your feelings *before* these fear-filled events happen. When you relate to fear proactively through these conversations, you bring strength and trust into your relationship to counter the fear's negative energy. You are familiarizing yourself, family members, and friends with advanced Decision Vision skills. With this tool, you can demonstrate your ease with a new approach to fear, displacing paralysis with strategy, insecurity with confidence.

Before trying to explain to others what you are doing, though, spend enough time with this tool to become familiar with it and how it works. Start with simple challenges and build from there, and practice gradually and gently. Use the torque generated by honesty to dislodge the footings of fear. One more thing: Relax. You are safe here—safe enough to make mistakes and try again.

Tool School Topic and Exercise #1: Fear Vortex

First, recall a highly charged, fear-filled event. Looking at the chart, try to locate this event within the upper region or lower region by asking yourself if this event involved a *necessary fear* or an *unnecessary fear*. You can tell the difference by examining the greater impact your behavior had on you or on another person's life. For example, fear about making your mortgage payments (or even making monthly rent payments) is a common concern. Thus most people would locate that fear in the *necessary fear* portion of the chart. On the other hand, fear about the success of a long-planned vacation may fit within the *unnecessary fear* realm since the consequence of that event may not spill into the future with adverse affects. Disappointing? You bet. Life altering? Probably not.

Next, look at the left and right sides of the chart. Consider which specific aspects of this fear-filled event you may be able to change and which aspects you cannot change. Let's return to the example about paying mortgage or rent. Since you may not be able to control inflation or even your job security, you could list this in the *things I cannot change* quadrant. Now look at the space reserved for things you can change. (Let's get creative here!) You may be able to control upgrading your insulation to save on heating bills or picking up some freelance work every once in a while to supplement your income. List all these possibilities—even the outrageous ones—within the *things I can change* quadrant. Make room for possibilities in this space.

Now return to the long-planned vacation example. In this case, consider what aspects you can control and which ones you cannot. You could list something like poor weather in the *things I cannot change* quadrant, while planning for indoor activities would be listed under *things I can change*.

Fear Vortex

Necessary Fear + **Things I cannot change −**	**Necessary Fear +** **Things I can change +**
Unnecessary Fear − **Things I cannot change −**	**Unnecessary Fear −** **Things I can change +**

How did you do? This is only the first of 12 simple exercises that will allow you to practice a friendlier, more relaxed approach to fear that will advance and possibly revise your current understanding. This book organizes the strands of your living fears—strands that appear in your dreams and memories. They are powerful perceptions of your own emotional world and a testament to your behavior in difficult circumstances.

Although this is serious business, remember to have fun as you work through these pages. Not all of the exercises are designed to be difficult. In fact, most of them encourage you to revise history and create a more satisfying ending that should make you smile. This will prepare you for the new life you are creating as you re-assert control over the emotion of fear. The benefits of practicing well-balanced emotional nutrition are similar to those of eating a well-balanced diet: strength, vitality, and happiness.

Chapter 3

Reclaiming Lost Property

"Mommy, what does it mean to suffer?"
—Emma Caitlin, age 7

This is where I began my journey. It was a Sunday afternoon in February 2006. My daughter Emma and I were eating lunch at a sandwich shop in a strip mall not far from our church, St. Thomas More, in Chapel Hill. The pastor of this remarkable faith family, Father John Durbin, had welcomed us warmly when we moved to town. Soon, I had volunteered as an assistant faith development teacher.

The Lenten season had begun and in preparation for Easter, Emma and her classmates were learning about the way Christ died. We used a helpful teacher's guidebook that talked about the crucifixion. I could tell by Emma's silence in the car after class that she found the story disturbing. She could recognize violence and grew sad. I tried to redirect her to the joyful season of Easter, but she remained distracted.

Just about every Sunday, after faith development class, Emma and I would be too hungry to wait until we got home to eat lunch, so we'd stop at this sandwich place before heading back to Hillsborough. After we'd pick up our sandwiches, chips, and drinks, we'd made our way to the front of the restaurant. On this particular Sunday, we found our favorite high-top table by the window open. Emma preferred this spot over the other tables because it was where the sun was streaming in. She sat with her back to the window, letting sunshine warm her as much as the hot cocoa she was sipping. I sat facing her, squinting into the bright light and shifting between the shady spots made by the "Kids Eat Free Tuesday Nights" posters. We had just settled in, and I was reaching for the condiment cup of ketchup when Emma asked me about suffering.

I have never been skillful at dodging my daughter's questions. As soon as the words left her mouth, my eyes were searing with tears that soon ran down my cheeks. Where do I begin? I wondered. Didn't she remember all my IVs and the multiple-site biopsies? No, not really. At the time that was going on two years previously, Emma had been only five, mercifully unaware of the danger stage-three cancer ushers in. My voice was locked inside my throat and, yes, people were beginning to stare. "I need to get better at this," I thought to myself. "Emma deserves it." Unheeded emotions bubble up at inconvenient times, don't they? "Note to self: Try to manage these unheeded feelings in private to avoid this public display in the future."

The following exercise can help you learn to do just that. In it, you will discover why suffering and fear are linked, and you'll learn how to break them apart decisively—and keep them apart.

Exercise #2: When I was and wasn't afraid

List three examples of times in your life when you were afraid. Don't limit yourself to the recent past. Try to recall the most fear-filled memories.

1. _____
2. _____
3. _____

Now give three examples of times when you didn't feel afraid, but looking back—you should have been!

1. _____
2. _____
3. _____

Exercise #3: Someone who wasn't afraid

Fill in the blank:

"The person I remember most who should have been afraid but wasn't is _____."

Think about that person, who may not necessarily have been a grown up, and imagine the feelings he or she had when experiencing the fearful event. How do his or her responses differ from yours? If you could ask this person how he or she confronted the situation, what do you think the answer would be?

_____
_____
_____

After working on this exercise, you have begun to assemble memories that shape your experience with fear. In the next chapter, you will begin to examine memories that explore situations where running away seemed to be the only solution.

Chapter 4

Running Away: Why Beginnings and Endings Look Alike

In this chapter, you will practice how to navigate detachment gently as you describe times that you remember running away—not only literally, but also figuratively. Consider running away to include declined invitations, unsent letters, or possibly unspoken conversations. The point of this next exercise is to build your skills in assessment and practice detachment as you commit your assessments to writing.

Until you learn to confront the truth about a situation and the fear it provokes, you will never be able to accept it—not to mention find the courage to interrupt it and move beyond it. This is why for many of us, beginnings and endings look alike. But you can break this non-productive cycle by learning where the stress points are in your experience of running away. This exercise asks you to spend time reflecting on those stress points and to consider their effectiveness in your life now.

Exercise #4: When I ran away

Please complete the following sentences:

The last time I ran away from something was:

The first time I can remember when I ran away from something was:

The hardest time I ran away from something was:

Understanding what you now know using the **Fear Vortex** as a guide, re-live the experience and describe how you would behave today. You can write it down or draw it in sketch form and then act it out. Create understanding of your experience in an environment that feels safe.

I would not run away now because I now realize that...

Let's step out of the kitchen for a moment.

You are growing more aware of the influence fear holds in your life as you continue your journal entries. The next exercise is a departure from recalling highly emotionally charged events. The exercise you're about to do invites you to describe a time when you kept fear in healthy check and were able to achieve an objective.

Chapter 5

Fear as a Neutral Partner

We've all had times when running away appeared to be the *only* available exit strategy. However, it's easy to get caught in that pattern of thinking. "Well, if running away worked once before," we ponder, "perhaps it will work again!"

Do you remember the lesson in fear mythology about confusing avoidance with safety? This is the emotional geography that leads to that emotional confusion. In any given situation, multiple strategies exist for navigating around a fear-filled situation. Habit tends to be an efficient short cut to success; however, it can also block our ability to seek a new approach.

The following exercise asks you to consider times when you were successful at moving beyond fear to neutralize its impact on your behavior. This exercise organizes your memories so that you can recognize the common ground shared among these successful experiences with fear.

At this point, you are ready to adopt a fresh approach to fear, synthesizing the lessons you already know. Now you can begin to replace less effective reactive strategies with more effective pro-active behaviors. Developing a stronger sense of what to anticipate is one of the many benefits this chapter promises to deliver. Reclaiming lost confidence is another.

Exercise #5: When I've overcome my fears

Below, list some examples when you (or someone you know) overcame fear. For some of you, it may be easier to share a story about another person's ability to neutralize fear to achieve an objective. For others, this exercise is a delicious recollection of sweet success. Either way, the object is for you to begin to relive the feelings associated with neutralizing fear.

What were the circumstances of these events? How long did it take to overcome fear? Were you alone, or did someone or something help you? Have you thought about this incident recently, or is it a deep memory? If you had to dredge this memory up, did you bury it deliberately, or did you just forget about it?

Memory A

_____
_____
_____
_____
_____
_____
_____

Memory B

_____
_____
_____
_____
_____
_____
_____

You are now actively developing new pathways to manage fear. This process requires you to develop the ability to see yourself as different—stronger and more experienced. Be gentle with yourself; you're taking a significant step toward growth. Leave behind any sense of shame or guilt. There is no room in this process for judgment. Give yourself adequate space to grow. Mercy spawns learning.

In the next sections, you will need to use your imagination. Daydreaming about experiences prepares us for future events. Acknowledge your past behavior, then review your new fear-navigation skills. Consider a new dynamic in which *you have the power to neutralize your fears* as if you were waving a magic wand.

With that in mind, how would you act in the fear-filled circumstances you described in the previous chapter about when you ran away from fear? What would you say and to whom would you say it? What would you do differently? How would others react to you?

_____
_____
_____
_____
_____
_____
_____
_____
_____

Before continuing....

Is it our belief in angels or our openness to extreme intervention that creates the space for miracles? Miracles needs space to live in, but what creates this space? Faith? A belief system? Dreams? Never forget your power to create a dream. Learn to let loose the bonds of rational thought. When we sleep, we are better able to see things that our living, waking minds with their rational filters obscure. Turn off those filters now, *before* you move on to the next exercises.

Chapter 6

Recognizing Intuition: Staging a Rebel-ution

Fear co-opts our ability to trust. The relationship we build between trust and ourselves forms the contours of *all* relationships we enter into, including relationships with family, friends, and co-workers. We also learn how to build trust with our talents. How can trust and the hope it implies influence present behaviors?

Trust helps by both establishing and re-affirming our present-day choices. We do this all day long without thinking about it. For example, you trust that the scientific, medical community is right about the dangers of smoking, so you decide to give up cigarettes. Trust encourages us to stick by our decisions, even through trying times. Marriage embodies this form of trust. Parenting does, too!

How can you improve your ability to trust yourself:

- with abundance?
- with responsibility?
- with your own creative powers?

In short, how can you practice trust? Rare is the person who has not met disappointment masquerading as misplaced trust. Often we experience this painful lesson as we try to figure out why friends sometimes say painful things about us behind our backs. The damage that results from these experiences hardens a person and teaches him or her to be more careful the next time. In your life, has misplaced trust and the disappointment that ensues made you stop trusting altogether? Have you silently ceded your own personal power to assess risk and to make your own decisions? This exercise will help you remember the times when you listened to your intuition successfully.

Fear of making mistakes and feeling foolish converge in a riptide that threatens to drown your core confidence. Fear can thwart your ability to grow by seeding self-limiting beliefs about yourself. Without care and diligently seeking out opportunities to practice judgment, these self-limiting beliefs cement you to a lifestyle and mindset that diminish you over time. What can you do to make yourself shrink-proof? Practice intuition.

The next exercise asks you to write about the moments in your life when you resisted outside sources of information and trusted your gut. Think about the times when your instincts proved right. The point of this exercise is to recall and to celebrate these occasions. Re-capture the feeling of that success. Ask yourself, "How did I feel? Happy? Affirmed? Confident? Lucky?"

When you finish the exercise, spend some time investigating where, at this point in your life, your instincts are pointing. Push back fear, just enough to visualize succeeding again. As you plot your course, can you see any way to recruit fear to help you? Perhaps fear marks boundaries that contain your comfort zone. This exercise can help you investigate an alternative approach that helps balance your need to proceed with caution (for example, a carefully crafted exit strategy) with your need to explore new opportunities.

Exercise #6: When I trusted my gut

Write about two times when you started to look for something that you thought you would never find. What prompted you to start? Were you successful or did you give up? Your example does not need to be a big event. The importance of this exercise is to ask yourself when was the last time you defied your rational voice and followed your instincts, which proved correct. Document that experience below.

Episode #1

_____
_____
_____
_____
_____
_____
_____
_____

Episode #2

_____
_____
_____

_____

_____

_____

_____

_____

How does it feel to actively practice intuition? Throughout the next few days, consider the opportunities you may have to exercise this gift. It may be as simple as choosing the quickest checkout line in the supermarket. Whatever the occasion, situations present ample chances for you to encounter intuition. Take small steps first. Grow more comfortable with your own skill, and gradually you may discover that your intuition about certain aspects of a situation is very strong.

Practicing listening to your intuition can help point you toward realizing a long-held goal. This exercise prepares you for the next, where you will revise history and put your design skills to the test.

Chapter 7

Create a Happy Ending: Dreamspace Destiny Calls

For many people, education and learning is all about memorizing facts. The truth is that as valuable as that skill is, it simply can't replace imagination. Imagination is not just a plaything. It's actually a form of intellect that helps craft our vision of the world we live in. Without this gift, your vision flattens and all the analytical powers of the world cannot hoist you above the everyday fray. Only imagination can help you build hope and restore trust.

Exercise #7: My happy ending

This exercise should be fun because it allows you to experience what it is like to be in control of your fears. In the space below, write a story, real or imaginary, that ends like this: "…and after that, I was no longer afraid."

_____

_____

_____

_____

_____

_____

_____

_____ and after that, I was no longer afraid.

Designing a life where fear's reach is curtailed may help you see the value of learning healthy fear-navigation skills. Remember, your emotions influence your behavior. I hope this exercise provided you with an example of how it feels to partner with fear and achieve an objective.

The next chapter describes how we use language to frame our feelings about fear-filled events. Since emotions impact actions, it may make sense to learn how to diffuse emotion through language.

Chapter 8

Framing Feelings in Language

In this chapter, you will learn how to organize your fear vocabulary and then sort through the impact these words have on your feelings. For many people, this is their favorite exercise because it strikes at the heart of all of their fear-filled experiences. Words have the power to influence your mind and thus, your behavior. Once you put your fear vocabulary down in writing, the power of those words fades. After this exercise, you may feel the ground shift. Closely held beliefs about yourself and your own powers will be called into question as they undergo a dramatic revision, thanks to some synonym synergy.

Exercise #8: Synonym synergy

How many words can you find that describe fear? If you need some help, go to a thesaurus. (If you don't happen to own one, you can find one online.) Becoming familiar with these words will be useful as you advance in this process. This will equip you with a clearer, more precise definition of your actual experiences with fear. The more precise you are now, the more exacting your tools for disengagement will become later.

I've started you off here with three words that describe fear. Now it's your turn:

Frightened   _____

Scary   _____

Creepy   _____

_____   _____

_____   _____

_____   _____

_____   _____

Are there any words you found in the thesaurus that you don't know?

Think about the words you wrote down. Which ones make you cringe? Which ones make you laugh? Re-organize your list, sorting their meaning from mildest to most powerful.

Mild:

_____

_____

_____

_____

_____

More powerful:

_____
_____
_____
_____
_____
_____

Most powerful:

_____
_____
_____
_____
_____

Was this re-organizing difficult for you? If it was, have you ever thought about the language of fear and the way we label our fears? Where did those labels come from?

Do you think you could re-arrange a new list of fears and sort them in a different way? What way would hold the most meaning for you?

Let me make a suggestion. Try to organize the same words in a way that mimics chronological development, like this:

Childhood fears:

_____
_____

_____

Young adult fears:

_____
_____
_____

Middle-age fears:

_____
_____
_____

Older years fears:

_____
_____
_____

Are the words you chose to describe your feelings interchangeable? Does your list include re-appearing words or experiences?

My mother used to have a recurring nightmare. She would dream that someone was chasing her down a dark alley. In her dream, she always managed to escape. Another common thread was that my mom was always in the same set of circumstances: She was running from someone at night and had a difficult time seeing who it was and where she was running.

The mornings after she'd had the nightmare, my mother would speak about her dream with my sister, brother, and me. Some mornings she would use the word "creepy" or phrases like "deathly afraid" to describe her feelings, but her story was always the same. She reported that although her pursuer never caught her, she was very scared. Even though it must have been difficult for her to re-live the dream the next day, by sharing her fear-filled experience, she taught us how to talk about fear—and that even moms can get scared.

Your improved language skills can diffuse emotionally charged experiences and will assist you into the next stage of Friendly Fear: fear location. In the next chapter, you will learn how to locate fear within your mind *and* within your body.

Chapter 9

Fear Location and Collateral Recovery

This chapter presents you with an opportunity to build your own timeline with fear. In earlier chapters, you assembled your history with fear. This exercise builds upon the assembly technique and asks you to consider *where* you choose to store these fear-filled memories. Talk about up close and personal!

Let me explain *why* you need to investigate this aspect of your experience with fear. In the rush to avoid painful memories, many people store these experiences in places where they don't belong. Feelings bubble up, and in the interest of expediency, we stuff them back down. Instead of heeding their warning, we try to hide from them. Sound familiar? In extreme cases, men and women ransom their own health to support a denial mechanism hungry for space and emotional energy. That can be a heavy concept to contemplate, and you may need a breather here.

Let's step out of the kitchen for a moment.

This chapter asks a simple question: Where does your fear live? As soon as you *discover* its favorite hiding place, you will be able to *recover* the space that it has consumed in your life. This chapter lets you play the role of collateral recovery specialist and reclaim the emotional energy you need to grow.

You begin this exercise by thinking about where your fear lives. For some of us, it's a tightness in our chest. For others, it's a knot in our stomach. In extreme cases, cases where physical danger is very possible, fear may present as a bitter taste in your mouth. However you encounter fear, this will help restore your ability to recognize it and to practice effective techniques to observe it, to measure it, and then to diffuse it.

Exercise #9: Where my fear lives

Where do your fears live? Do they hide deep down in your gut? Are they buried in your too-busy-to-think head? Or do they live with you front and center—never out of sight?

My fears live:

_____
_____
_____

Next, consider where fear lives in your personal timeline. Are you more afraid of the past, present, or future? Can you distinguish how time affects your fears? Have they grown with time? Have they diminished over time? Fears about the future can be emotionally draining because they have the greatest unknown shadows to their makeup. Below, write about where in your timeline you feel your greatest fears live and thrive:

If you could extinguish one of your fears at any point in your fear timeline, which one would it be? (Please choose only one.)

Now finish the following statement: "I chose this fear because if it were gone, I would be able to ...."

This exercise has prepared you for the next chapter, which probes the connection we all make both consciously and unconsciously between fear and intention by awakening your own practiced detachment and observation skills.

Chapter 10

The Intention of Fear: Shining Your Fear Flashlight

With this chapter, you delve deeper still into your relationship with fear. But before you begin, I want to emphasize this critical truth: **The honesty that you bring into these last few exercises is vital to achieving the level of Friendly Fear skills you will need to strengthen your decision-making skills.** Don't take these words lightly!

Decision Vision applies emotional savvy fueled by truthful observations. Handling your emotions with honesty is often painful. But when you learn from your experience, pain plays a central role to your emotional growth. On the other hand, when you neglect to learn from painful experiences, you unwittingly create circumstances that resist healing and that perpetuate suffering. Choose wisely.

Let's step out of the kitchen for a moment.

Deciphering the intention of your fears forms the basis for this chapter, which challenges you to set the record straight using incisive honesty to confront fears in the comfort and safety of your notebook.

Like a flashlight, this exercise helps bring light into those hard-to-reach spaces where memories languish. Here, you will learn how to align your Friendly Fear skills with *honesty*. Ideas have expiration dates. Values do not. As you consign fear to a lesser role in your life, you will have more space to devote to honesty. Honesty diffuses fear because it rises above pretense and calls into question the very essence of fear's energy: ignorance.

Exercise # 10: My Fear Flashlight

Are you able to decipher the intention of your fear? For example, could you fill in the blank in this sentence: "This made me frightened because I thought I would become _____."

Think about the last paragraph you wrote in the previous chapter, and then comment below on how you would complete the above sentence:

_____
_____
_____
_____

At this point, you may need a break from heavy lifting for a bit. The next chapter is an abrupt departure from your work in building a personal narrative with fear. It invites you to consider two very distinct feelings and dares you to compare the emotional charge each feeling bears.

Chapter 11

Parallel Experiences, Congruent Lessons

Are you ready to explore an improbable association? The whole point of this chapter is to help you see with fresh eyes the beauty and promise planted within most fear-filled situations. Leave your feelings of regret behind. As with all chapters found in this book, there's no space for judgment here.

The exercises below are all about exploring alternative responses in the safety of your own journal. Give yourself permission to try a new approach to a fear-filled situation. The lesson here is simple. Keeping what you have learned so far in the forefront of your mind, indulge in a crazy compare-and-contrast game. This may be difficult at first, because I am asking you to suspend all rational thinking and play with a critical part of your mind—your imagination. Yet the imagination is precisely where all healing begins.

Exercise #11: How I feel about falling…in love and in fear

Compare your feelings about these two statements:

I am in love.

I am in fear.

How do they make you feel and behave? How do others behave toward you once you have expressed these feelings toward them? Remember to look for similarities—don't highlight only the differences. Write your thoughts below:

_____
_____
_____
_____
_____
_____
_____
_____
_____
_____

Imagination helps secure the space you need to reconcile the powerful emotion of fear within the entire array of human emotions. It does this by blurring the lines between experience (past) and anticipation (future).

Throughout this book, you have summoned your own history of fear-filled events and then written about these events. In many exercises, you had to revise the story's ending to reflect your new relationship with fear. In those exercise, I asked you to suspend reality and create endings to stories you had experienced that brought you a sense of closure and fulfillment.

The last exercise culminates your skills as an experienced journal writer. Here you blend Decision Vision skills with imagination to rewrite your personal narrative with fear and restore balance to your relationship with fear.

Chapter 12

Making Sense of It All: The Fear Factor

Fire consumes all things in its path. Love also behaves this way. Fear does, too. The point of all of these exercises is to help you take the first step in disengaging your **Fear Vortex**. Recognize the powerful energy associated with the feelings you find inside fear-filled situations. Divest the emotional distraction that fuels fear. Consign it to a lesser role in your decision-making. Befriend fear—do not try to destroy it.

Diverting energy away from fear can propel you to new heights and inspire you to keep growing—as long as it is harnessed effectively. Again, choose wisely. Fear unchecked can thwart growth. Unheeded, fear consumes precious emotional energy reserved for hope and vital for building trust. Listen to what fear is trying to tell you about yourself and about any given situation.

Consider many alternative responses to any fear-filled situation. Be open to your own intuitive understanding of the present fear-driven problem and let intuition harmonize with fear. Friendly Fear promises to keep you safe and alert. Just as you shouldn't overestimate fear, neither should you underestimate your own decision-making skills. Given the proper perspective and rigorous examination of alternative solutions, you will make well-balanced decisions and grow more confident with practice.

Ticket to Ride

Where do you go in your head when you start feeling frightened? I return to those places and events that I lived through during the period that I was frightened. Over time, I have learned how to keep my fears in check upon realizing that the event has already happened and nothing can bring it back to me. Or can it?

You can't really kill past events. You store them in your memory, where they can take on a life of their own. How you choose to integrate them into your daily life predicts how effectively you engage your world and develop into your best possible self. Isn't it odd how often some people choose to relive these painful, fear-filled experiences? It's as strange as continuing to hit your head against a brick wall. And by now, you know that instead of signing up for another headache, you can turn to some much more productive options—including fantasy.

Now, I am not suggesting getting lost in a fantasy world. *I am suggesting that you make imagination the center of your learning life.* The moment you realize that you are watching a past event flash in front of you is the very same moment you must turn on your dream channel. Focus to create new experiences on this page. Commit them to your living memory. Keep your *Friendly Fear Notebook* with you at all times so that you can filter in the new script and then...relax.

You have worked hard to rewrite the fear-filled event and you have created a new ending. You have learned how to amend your memory scrapbook. Now, when you come across a new incident revealing similar characteristics, call up the file—the one with the satisfying end—and hit the "play" button. Teach yourself how to develop a new response. Practice in moments of free time. Exert yourself!

Take a deep breath. Are you ready for the final exercise?

Exercise #12: My new history with fear

My rewritten fear history would go like this:

At one time, I was afraid of:

_____
_____
_____

Looking back, I realize that I had this fear because I:

_____
_____
_____

Now, I am now able to think about this fear differently. I can respond to the energy it exerts in my life by disabling its destructive force when I consider:

_____
_____

Because I have mastered this fear, I have become better at:

_____
_____
_____
_____
_____

I use the energy I once spent being frightened to become more (effective, creative, relaxed, confident, etc.):

_____
_____
_____

Congratulations! You knew this all along but needed a safe place to write it all down on paper so you could detangle the strands of your fears. Friendly Fear may take some time to master. But it's worth it. As you conclude this final exercise, you are well prepared to diffuse the emotional energy in any and all fear-filled situations and harness that energy to support more constructive behaviors—behaviors conducive to adaptation and growth.

Chapter 13

Point of Departure

One of fear's great enigmas is that it has the power to connect us with each other while, *at the same time*, to turn us inward. Music has that power too: We can sing together while privately reflecting upon the words and the melody of a song. We experience this without any sense of contradiction. Both fear and music exist comfortably between community and solitude.

So often in this digital age, our world can be reduced to simple binary code. For example, we either love something or hate something. Our perceptions have been built around these two switches: on and off. As children, we quickly learn to assess if something is good or bad. Implied in this reasoning is "all-good" and "all-bad." This way of thinking carries us into our adult lives and brings with it an implicit promise—as well as a danger.

The promise rests with the ease at which we can respond to the vast stimuli in our lives. Without much thinking, we can accept new information without feeling overwhelmed. It's almost pre-digested!

Science works this way, too. You may have heard the phrase "two standard deviations from the mean," which is a measure of the data's significance. When a study's findings fall between two standard deviations from the mean, they are rendered inconclusive and may not even be reported because the researchers would classify such findings as insignificant. In short, the experiment either worked or did not work. There's very little middle ground.

The danger inherent in approaching our world with a binary mindset is that it overlooks the possibility for situations to carry both "on" and "off" messages. And that limits both understanding and growth. After learning about Friendly Fear, you have a totally new appreciation for how fear brings both positive and negative energy with it. You now know how to leverage *both* qualities so that you can strengthen your decision-making skills.

My intention has been to encourage this inclusive, holistic type of thinking to take root within your soul. The Asian metaphor for life is represented in the yin and yang symbol, where creative and destructive forces not only coexist but actually give birth to one another. There is no "on" or "off" switch within this perception, and thus contradictions dissolve. This circular thinking can restore the balance between fear and growth.

As you've worked through *Friendly Fear Notebook*, you've gently morphed from reader into writer, learning to skillfully wrap your own words around your heart so that it feels safe and supported. From this place of safety, you've found the strength to gaze inward and see your Truth. But your journey need not end here. Like the ideas you've been practicing, the journey is a circular one: It works best if you come back to it again and again, continuing to bring yourself around to a new level of understanding.

Each time you pick up this book and work the exercises, you'll be covering new territory, continuing to move deliberately and gracefully between comfort and risk, crisis and recovery. I sincerely hope you enjoy the dance.

A final thought...

The only element that separates a queen bee from the drones and worker bees is the food she eats at birth. Your thoughts are your food. Choose wisely. Do not surrender yourself to other people's expectations. They will never fit you. Keep love in your life and stay focused on it. Be ruthless in seeking out the truth behind your fears, yet be gentle in your surrender to this knowledge. Grow. Put a friendly face on fear and vanquish self-doubt. You will always be a hero once you learn to love your fears.

Appendix A
Outline of Exercises

Chapter 1: How This Book Works

    Tool School topics

- The Fear-o-meter
- Sight Setting

Chapter 2: The Truth About Fear Mythology: Fears, Fables, and Falsehoods

    Tool School topics

- Privacy Contract
- My Friendly Fear Notebook's Title Page
- The Flip Side
- Fear Vortex (Exercise #1)

Chapter 3: Reclaiming Lost Property

    Exercise #2: When I was and wasn't afraid

- Times when I was afraid
- Times when I wasn't afraid but should have been

    Exercise #3: Someone who wasn't afraid

- The person I remember most who should have been afraid but wasn't is...

Chapter 4: Running Away: Why Beginnings and Endings Look Alike

Exercise #4: When I ran away

- The last time I ran away from something was...
- The first time I ran away from something was...
- The hardest time I ran away was...
- I would not run away now because I now realize that...

Chapter 5: Fear as a Neutral Partner

Exercise #5: When I've overcome my fears

- Memory A
- Memory B
- How I would now overcome the fear that caused me to run away

Chapter 6: Recognizing Intuition: Staging a Rebel-ution

Exercise #6: When I trusted my gut

- Episode #1
- Episode #2

Chapter 7: Create a Happy Ending: Dreamspace Destiny Calls

Exercise #7: My happy ending

- Write a story that ends with this phrase: "... and after that, I was no longer afraid."

Chapter 8: Framing Feelings in Language

Exercise #8: Synonym synergy

- Create a list of words that describe fear

- Sort the list from mild to most powerful
- Create your timeline using these fear adjectives

Chapter 9: Fear Location and Collateral Recovery

Exercise #9: Where my fears live

- My fears live…
- If I could extinguish one fear, it would be…
- I chose this fear because if it were gone, I would be able to…

Chapter 10: The Intention of Fear: Shining Your Fear Flashlight

Exercise #10: My Fear Flashlight

- This made me frightened because I thought I would become…

Chapter 11: Parallel Experiences, Congruent Lessons

Exercise #11: How I feel about falling…in love and in fear

- Compare and contrast your feelings about these two phrases: "I am in love" and "I am in fear"

Chapter 12: Making Sense of It All: The Fear Factor

Exercise #12: My new history with fear

- At one time I was afraid of…
- Looking back, I realize that I had this fear because I…
- I can respond differently by disabling its destructive force when I consider…
- Because I have mastered this fear, I have become better at…
- I use the energy I once spent being frightened to become more…

Appendix B
The Fear-o-meter

Here is another copy of **The Fear-o-meter** that you encountered in Chapter 1. You may wish to use this second copy after you've worked through all the exercises and have had time to integrate what you've learned. Comparing your answers here to the answers you gave initially will show you how you have updated your thoughts about and relationship with fear.

On a scale from 1 to 5, please circle your responses below according to the following guidelines:

1 = strongly agree

2 = somewhat agree

3 = neutral

4 = somewhat disagree

5 = strongly disagree

1. Fear is something I *rarely* talk about with friends or family.

    1   2   3   4   5

2. Journaling promotes self-awareness.

    1   2   3   4   5

3.   I don't know how or where to begin when it comes to talking about fear.

       1   2   3   4   5

4.   I would find it helpful if I had a method to help me talk about fear with my family, friends, and business associates.

       1   2   3   4   5

5.   I would be willing to spend time and money to improve my fear-navigation skills.

       1   2   3   4   5

Appendix C
Additional Resources for Further Help

For help locating mental health professionals or for information about mental health, contact:

American Psychiatric Association

www.psych.org

1000 Wilson Blvd., Suite 1825

Arlington, VA 22209-3901

(888) 357-7924 (888-35-PSYCH)

(703) 907-7300

American Psychological Association

www.apa.org

750 First St., NE

Washington, DC 20002-4242

(800) 374-2721

(202) 336-5500

National Alliance on Mental Illness

www.nami.org

3803 N. Fairfax Dr., Suite 100

Arlington, VA 22203

(800) 950-6264 (800-950-NAMI)

(703) 524-7600

To locate a professional life coach or business coach, contact:

Coaches Training Institute

www.thecoaches.com

4000 Civic Center Dr., Suite 500

San Rafael, CA 94903

(800) 691-6008

(415) 451-6000

International Coach Federation

www.coachfederation.org

2365 Harrodsburg Rd., Suite A325

Lexington, KY 40504

(888) 423-3131

(859) 219-3580

About the Author

Boston-born author Lee Anne McClymont earned a bachelor's degree in classical languages from Smith College and a Master of Healthcare Administration from Simmons College. She spent the next 15 years in New York City, building programs in cardiovascular services for one of the country's premier academic medical centers.

When she was 39 years old, married, and the mother of a five-year-old daughter, Lee Anne was diagnosed with stage-three non-Hodgkin's lymphoma. Within a matter of days, her world shifted from that of healthcare administrator to healthcare consumer. The aftermath of this experience led her to re-align her relationship with everything that mattered to her: God, country, and family.

In a two-year period, Lee Anne and her family journeyed through cancer, career loss, and a relocation to North Carolina. She captured the thread of her story in her private journal, *Sweet Potatoes*, a collection of questions that centered on the relationship she had with fear and its influence in her life. *Friendly Fear Notebook*, Lee Anne's first book, is a greatly expanded adaptation of that journal. Lee Anne also created the "Harness Fear, Harvest Hope" workshops to gently guide participants through the Friendly Fear program she outlines in this book.

Lee Anne lives in Hillsborough, NC, with her husband Bill, her daughter Emma, and the family's dog, Mango.

www.ingramcontent.com/pod-product-compliance
Ingram Content Group UK Ltd.
Pitfield, Milton Keynes, MK11 3LW, UK
UKHW041957230426
12048UKWH00008B/393